ZIGGY®

HOT OFF THE PRESSES

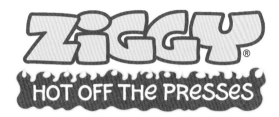

Recent *Ziggy* Books

Ziggy Comes Up Short
Ziggy's Friends for Life
Ziggy on Parade
Ziggy's Gift
Character Matters
Ziggy Goes Hollywood
The Zen of Ziggy
Get Ziggy with It
Ziggy's Divine Comedy

Treasuries

A Little Character Goes a Long Way
The First 25 Years Are the Hardest!
Ziggy's Star Performances

ZIGGY®

HOT OFF THE PRESSES

by Tom Wilson

Andrews McMeel
Publishing, LLC

Kansas City

ATTENTION: SCHOOLS AND BUSINESSES ---

Andrews McMeel books are available at quantity discounts with bulk purchase for educational, business, or sales promotional use. For information, please write to: Special Sales Department, Andrews McMeel Publishing, LLC, 1130 Walnut Street, Kansas City, Missouri 64106.

SIGH! YOU KNOW, FUZZ, IT SEEMS LIKE NOTHING LASTS FOREVER.
...FOR ALL OF HUMAN HISTORY CIVILIZATIONS RISE AND FALL, EMPIRES COME AND GO...
MOUNTAIN RANGES ARE BUILT UP AND GROUND TO DUST...
..ONLY THE SUN AND THE MOON CAN BE COUNTED ON TO RISE AND SET FOREVER!
PSSSSSSSIT
FWWEEE-ZZZ!!
..SO MUCH FOR 'FOREVER'!

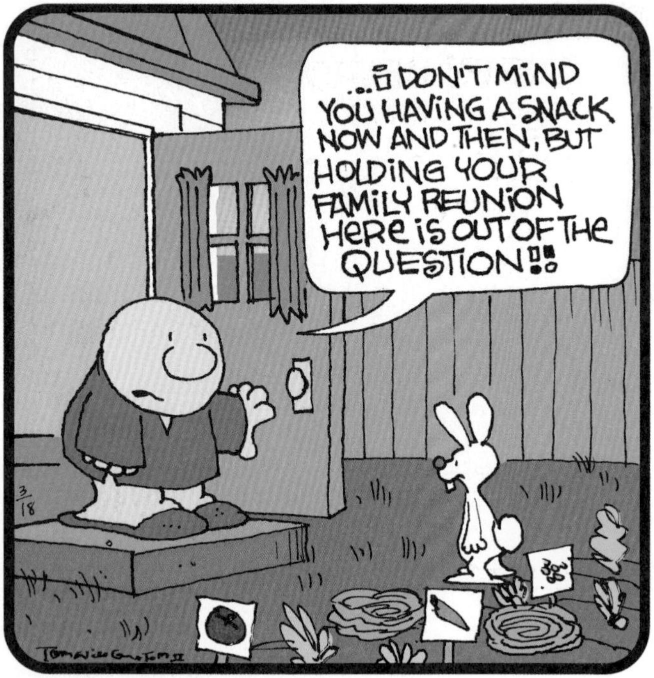
...I DON'T MIND YOU HAVING A SNACK NOW AND THEN, BUT HOLDING YOUR FAMILY REUNION HERE IS OUT OF THE QUESTION!!

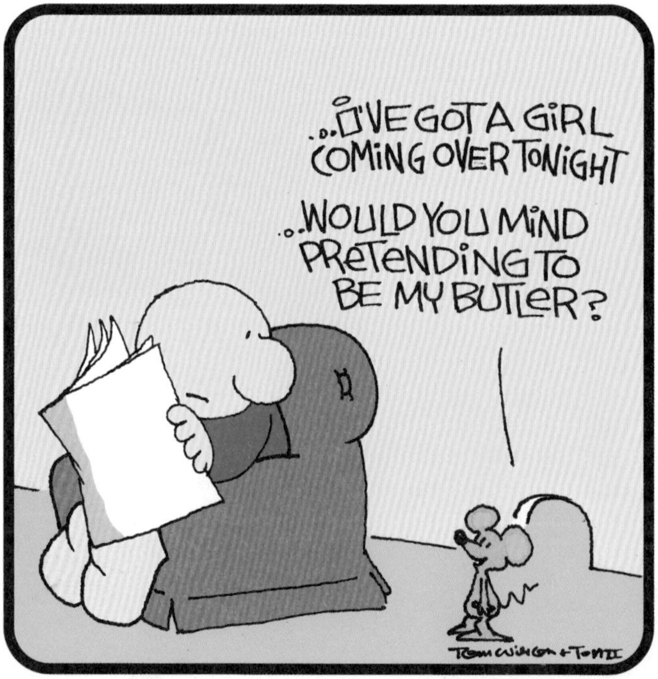
...I'VE GOT A GIRL COMING OVER TONIGHT
...WOULD YOU MIND PRETENDING TO BE MY BUTLER?

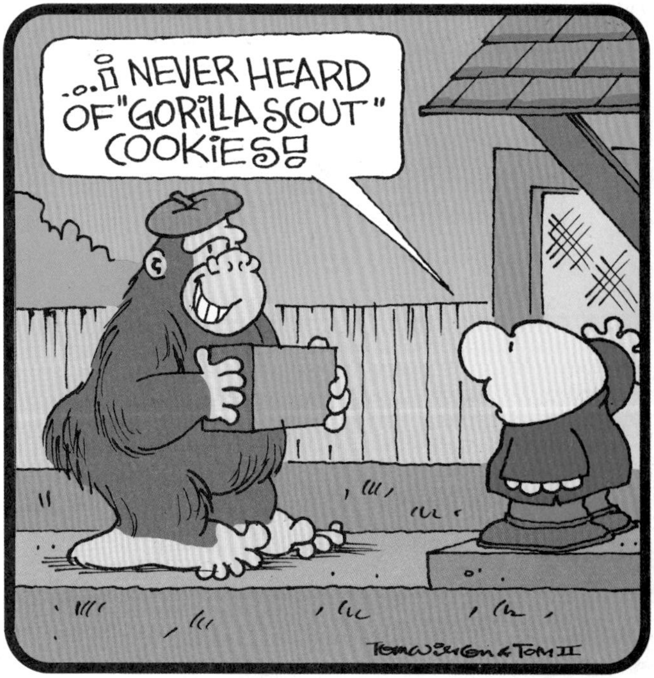
..I NEVER HEARD OF "GORILLA SCOUT" COOKIES!
Tom Wilson & Tom II

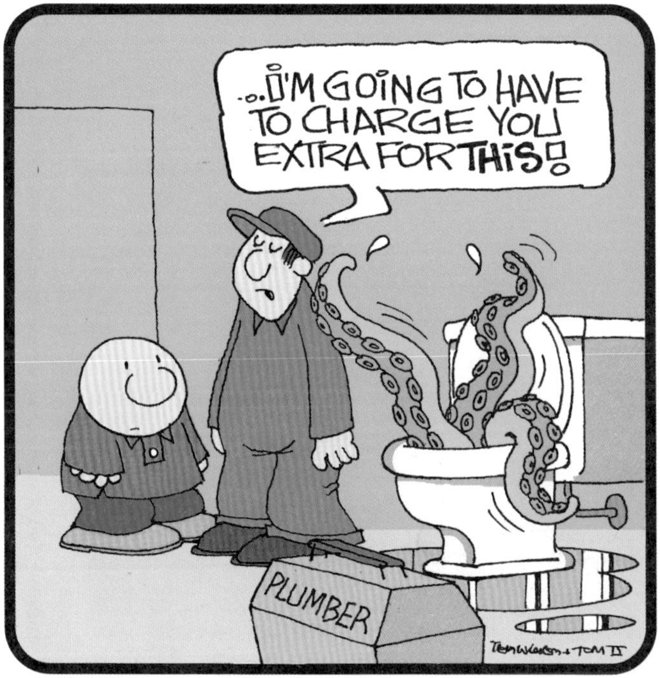
..I'M GOING TO HAVE TO CHARGE YOU EXTRA FOR THIS!
PLUMBER
Tom Wilson & Tom II

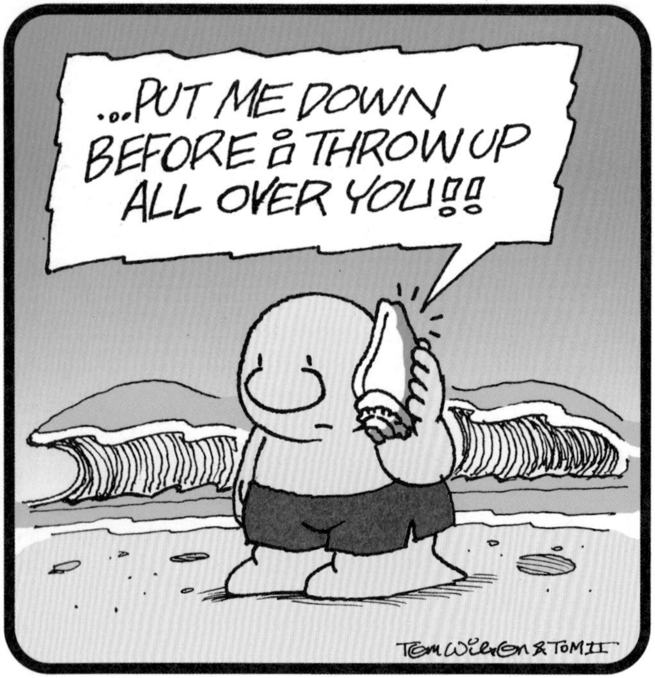
...PUT ME DOWN BEFORE I THROW UP ALL OVER YOU!!!
TOM WILSON & TOM II

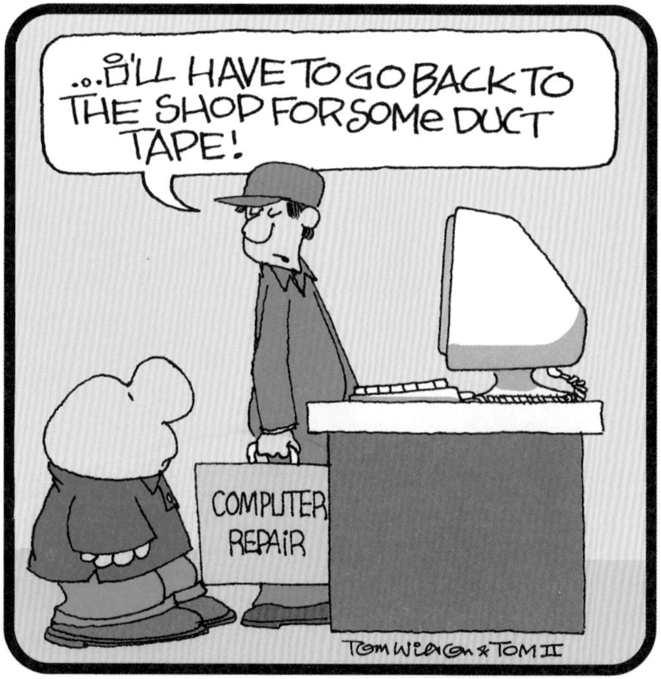
...I'LL HAVE TO GO BACK TO THE SHOP FOR SOME DUCT TAPE!
COMPUTER REPAIR
TOM WILSON & TOM II

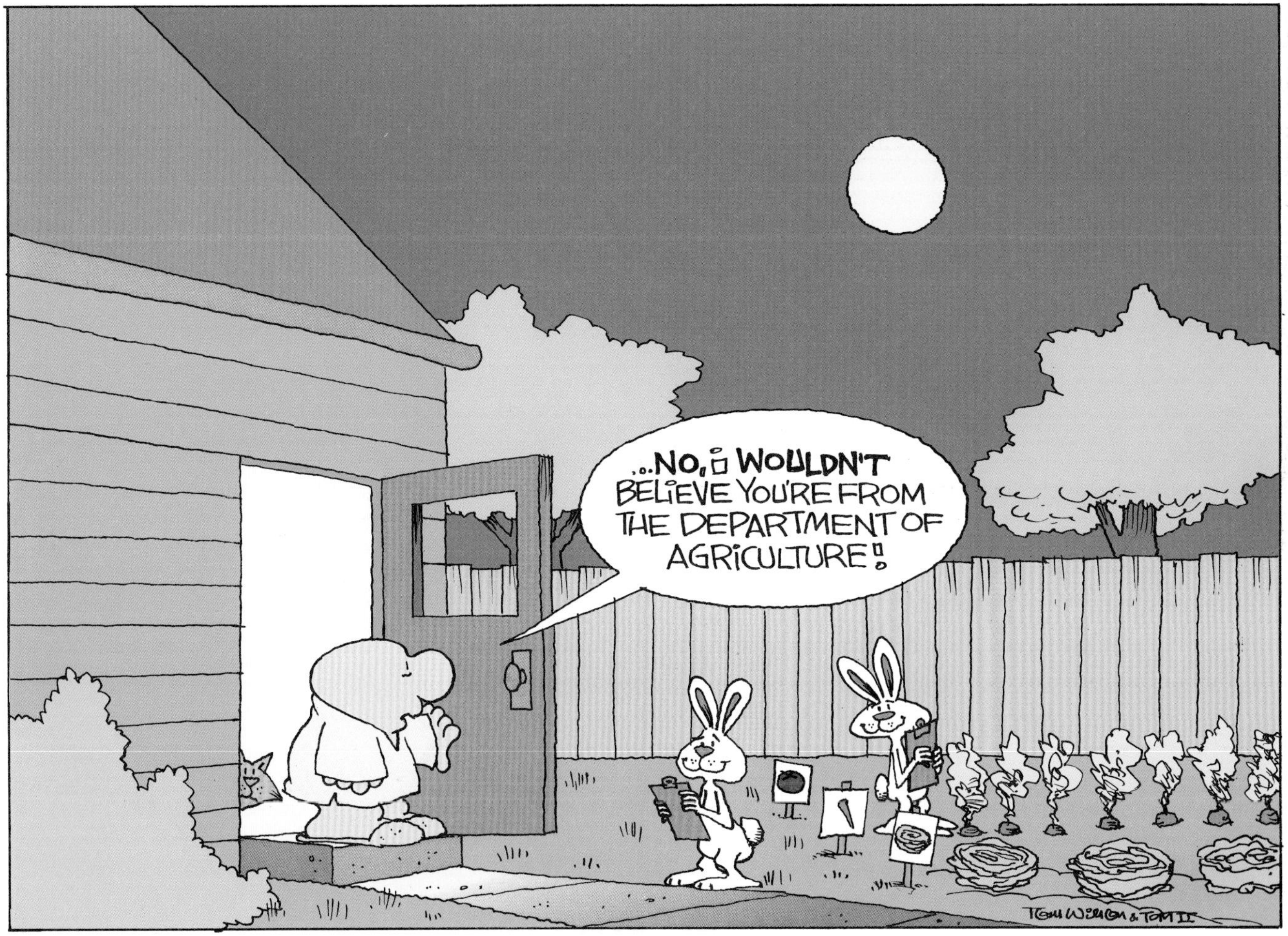
...NO, I WOULDN'T BELIEVE YOU'RE FROM THE DEPARTMENT OF AGRICULTURE!
TOM WILSON & TOM II

..WE'RE ALL GOING TO THE BEACH... ..YOU KNOW, THE GREAT BIG LITTER BOX!
Tom Wilson & Tom II

..COULD YOU ORDER SOMETHING ELSE, SIR? ..I DON'T FEEL VERY LOBSTERY TODAY!
SEAFOOD SHACK
Tom Wilson. Tom II

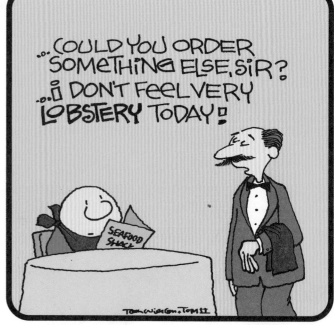

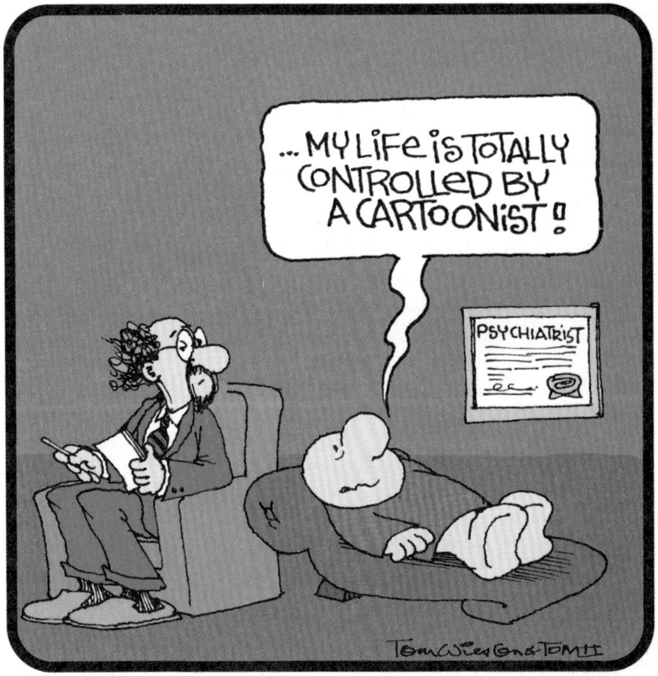
...MY LIFE IS TOTALLY CONTROLLED BY A CARTOONIST!
PSYCHIATRIST
TOM WILSON & TOM II

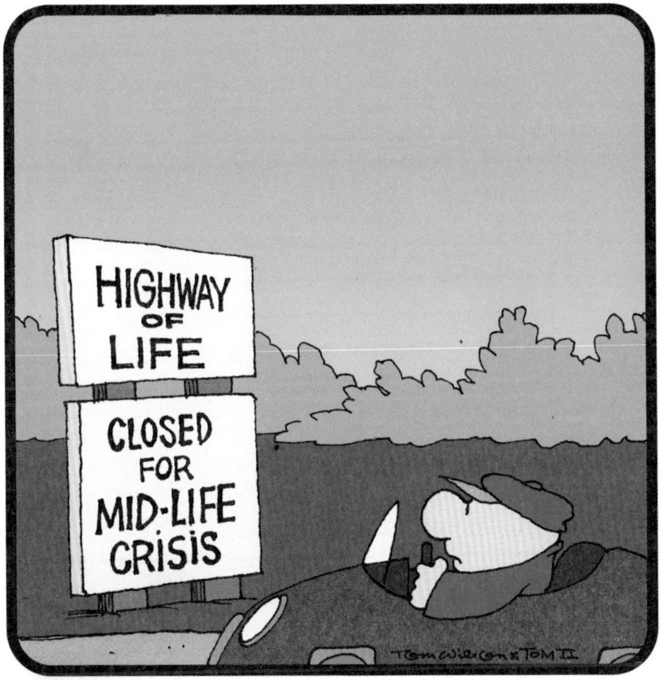
HIGHWAY OF LIFE
CLOSED FOR MID-LIFE CRISIS
TOM WILSON & TOM II

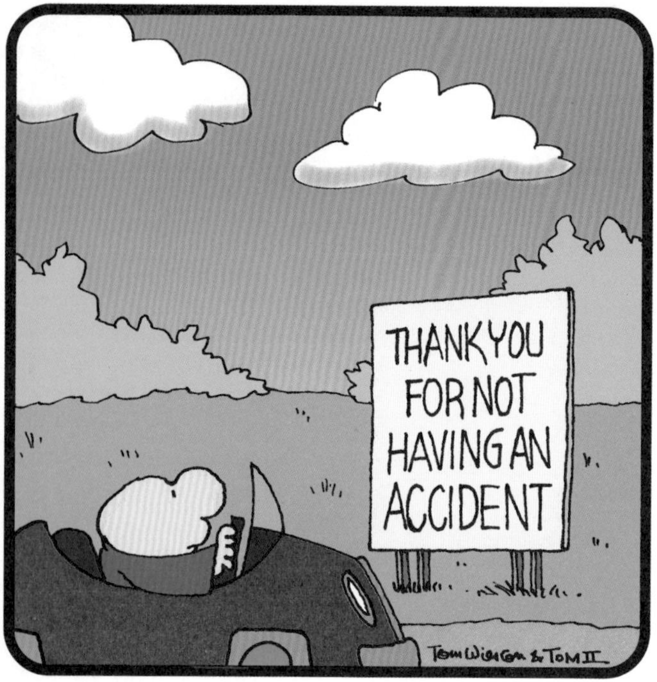
THANK YOU FOR NOT HAVING AN ACCIDENT
TOM WILSON & TOM II

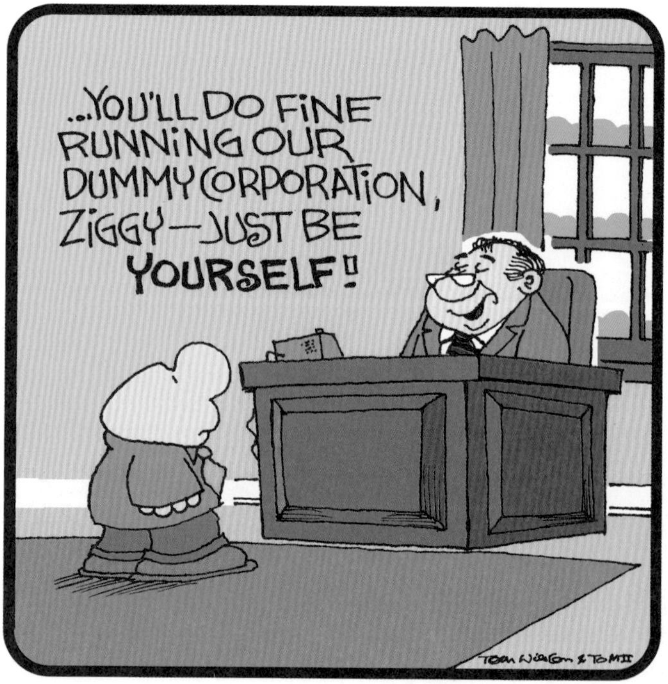
...YOU'LL DO FINE RUNNING OUR DUMMY CORPORATION, ZIGGY—JUST BE **YOURSELF!**
TOM WILSON & TOM II

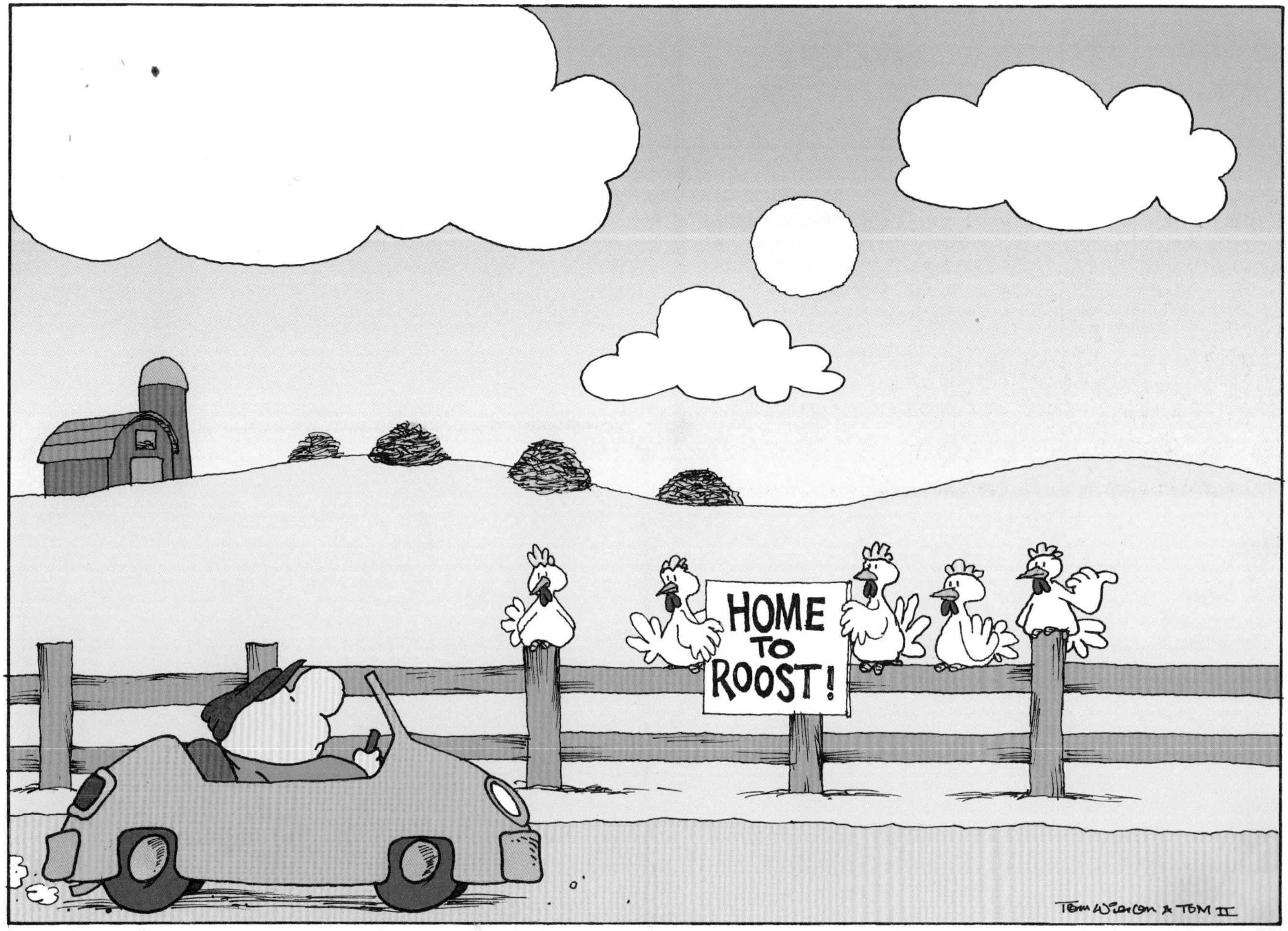
HOME TO ROOST!
TOM WILSON & TOM II

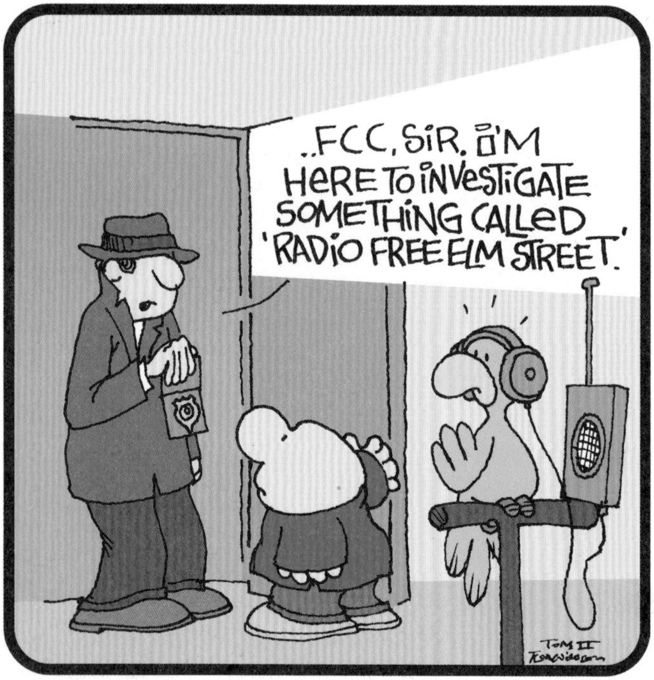
..FCC, SIR. I'M HERE TO INVESTIGATE SOMETHING CALLED 'RADIO FREE ELM STREET.'

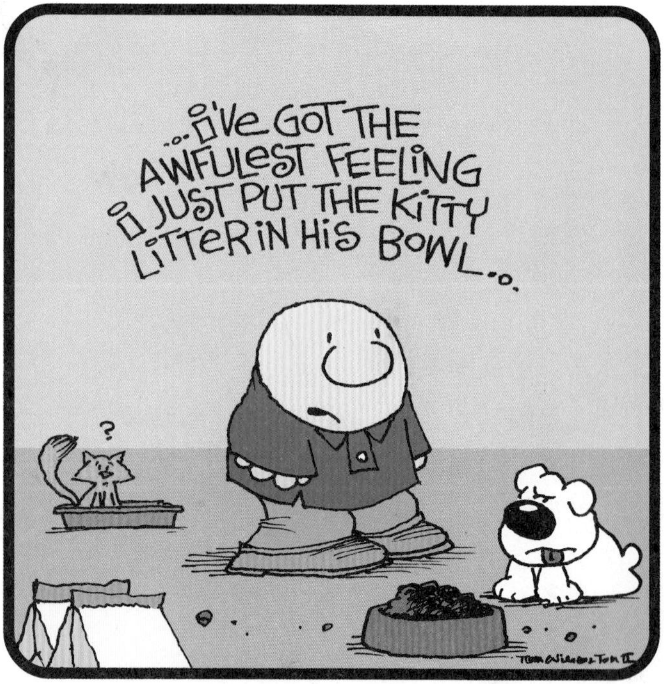
..o..I'VE GOT THE AWFULEST FEELING I JUST PUT THE KITTY LITTER IN HIS BOWL..o.
?

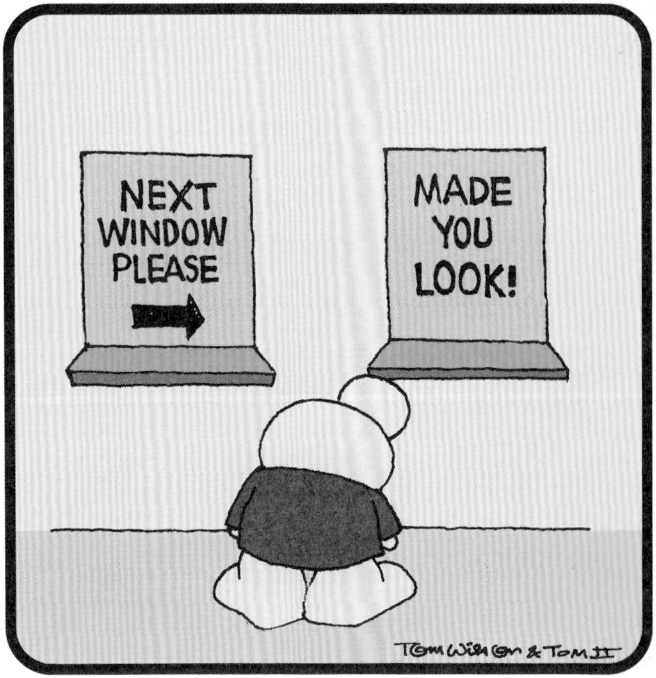
NEXT WINDOW PLEASE
MADE YOU LOOK!
TOM WILSON & TOM II

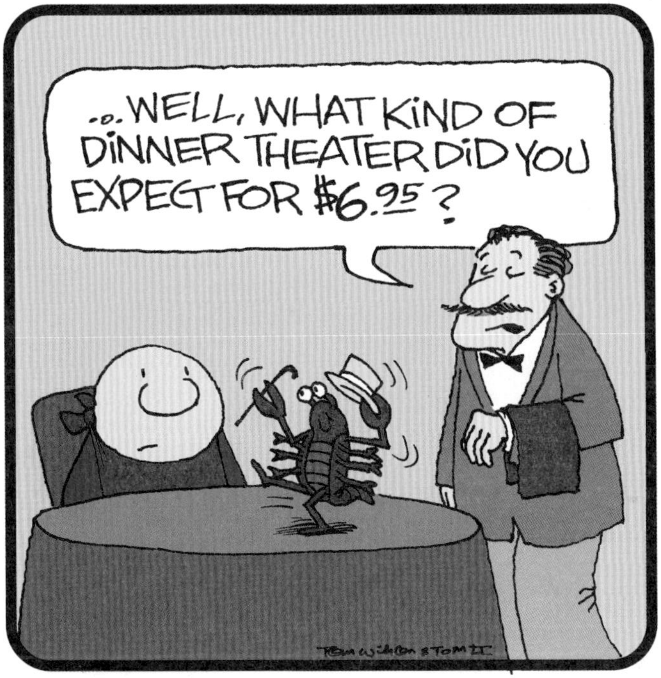
...WELL, WHAT KIND OF DINNER THEATER DID YOU EXPECT FOR $6.95?
TOM WILSON & TOM II

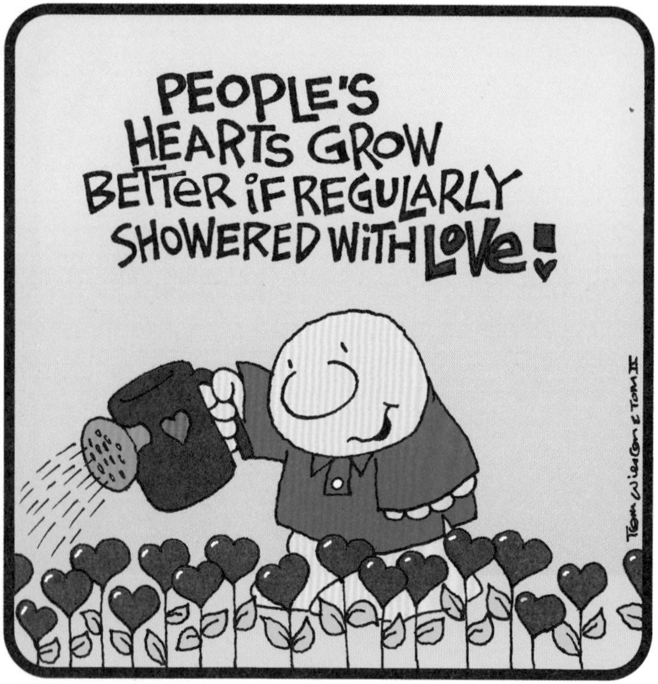
PEOPLE'S HEARTS GROW BETTER IF REGULARLY SHOWERED WITH LOVE!

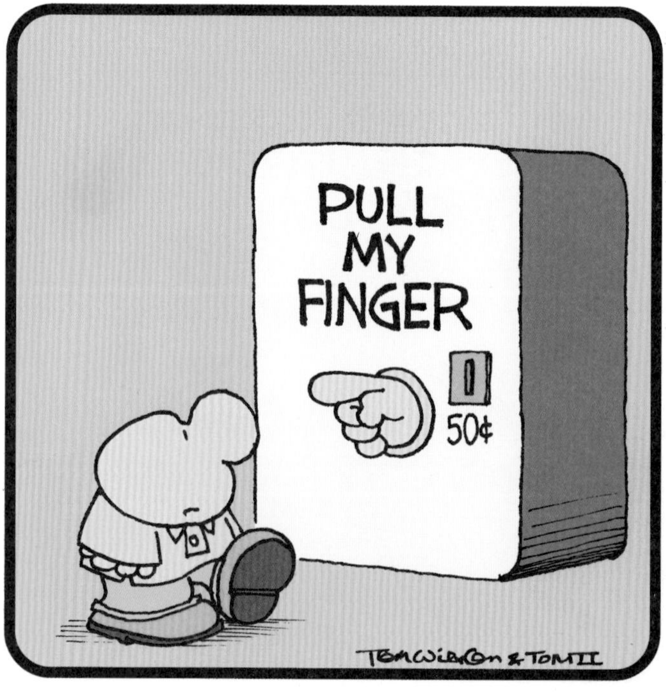
PULL MY FINGER
50¢

STARBUX
...HERE YOU GO, SIR.
ONE MOCHA CREME MINT APPLE-CINNAMON
..RASPBERRY TRUFFLE... CHOCOLATE CHIP CARAMEL...
OOPS
...I FORGOT TO PUT THE COFFEE IN!!

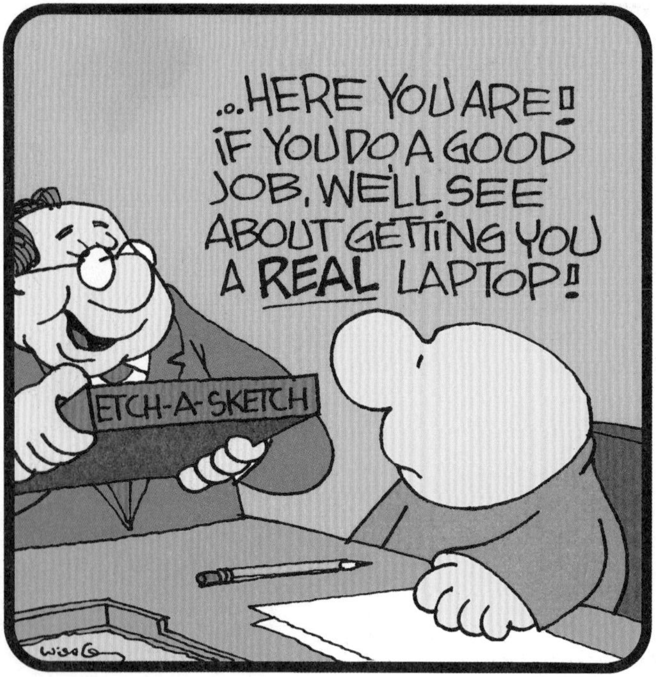

..HERE YOU ARE!
IF YOU DO A GOOD JOB, WE'LL SEE ABOUT GETTING YOU A REAL LAPTOP!
ETCH-A-SKETCH

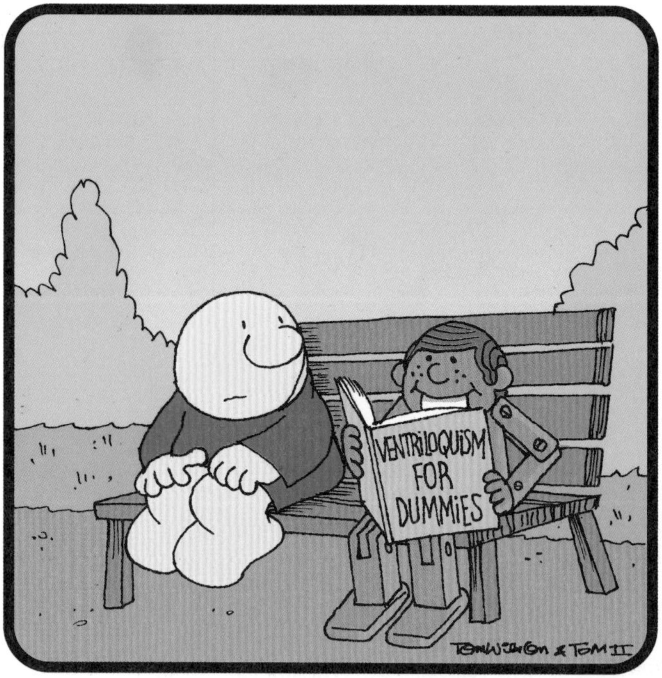

VENTRILOQUISM FOR DUMMIES
TOM WILSON & TOM II

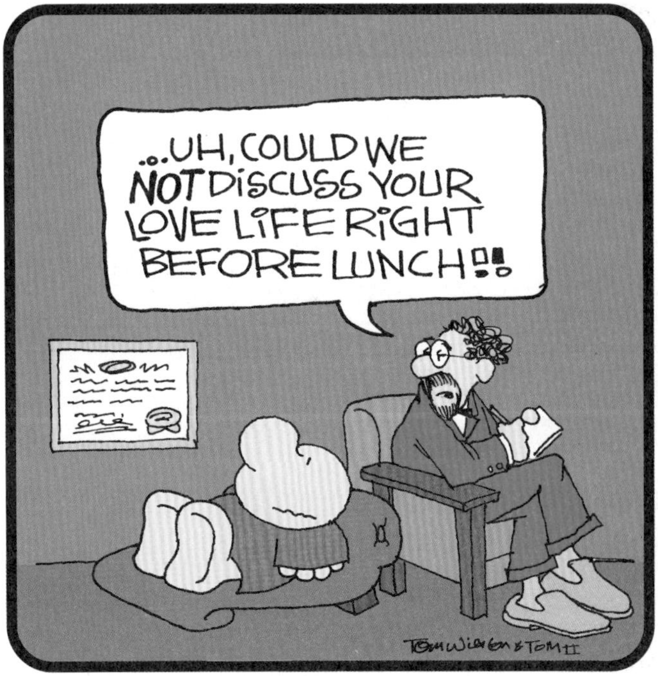
..UH, COULD WE NOT DISCUSS YOUR LOVE LIFE RIGHT BEFORE LUNCH!!
TOM WILSON & TOM II

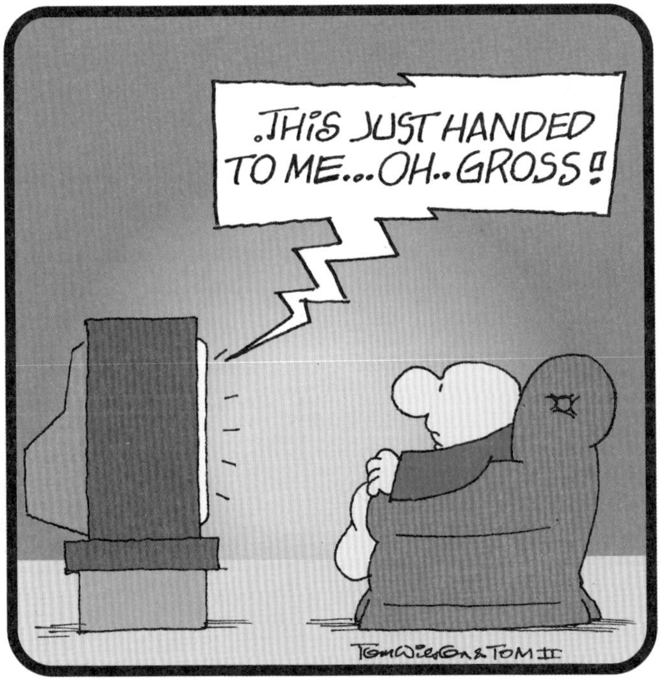
.THIS JUST HANDED TO ME...OH..GROSS!
TOM WILSON & TOM II

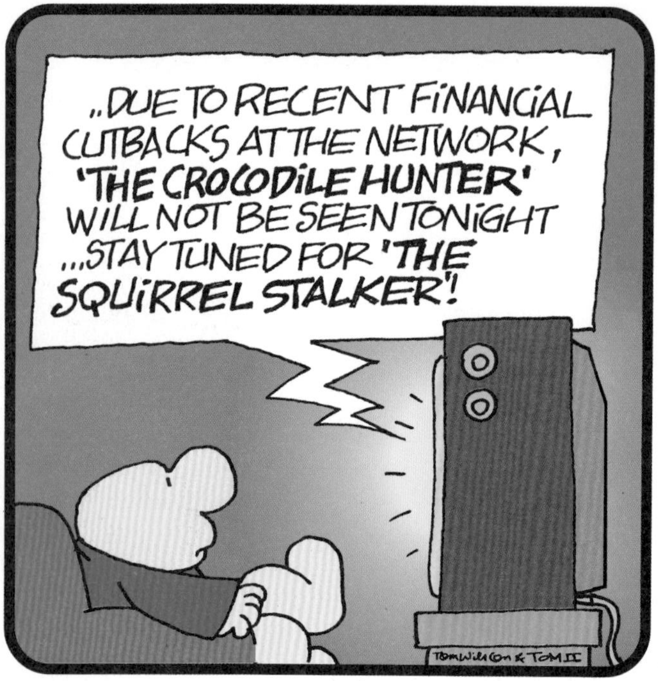
..DUE TO RECENT FINANCIAL CUTBACKS AT THE NETWORK, 'THE CROCODILE HUNTER' WILL NOT BE SEEN TONIGHT ...STAY TUNED FOR 'THE SQUIRREL STALKER'!
TOM WILSON & TOM II

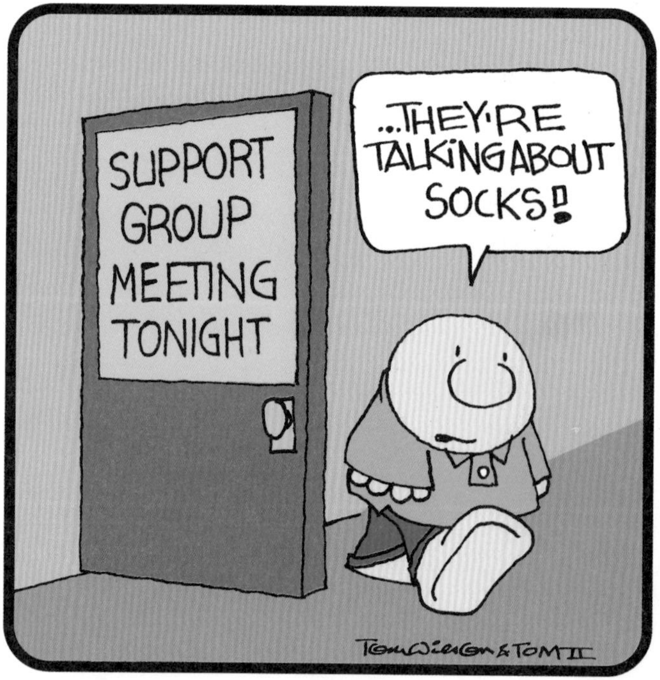
SUPPORT GROUP MEETING TONIGHT
...THEY'RE TALKING ABOUT SOCKS!
TOM WILSON & TOM II

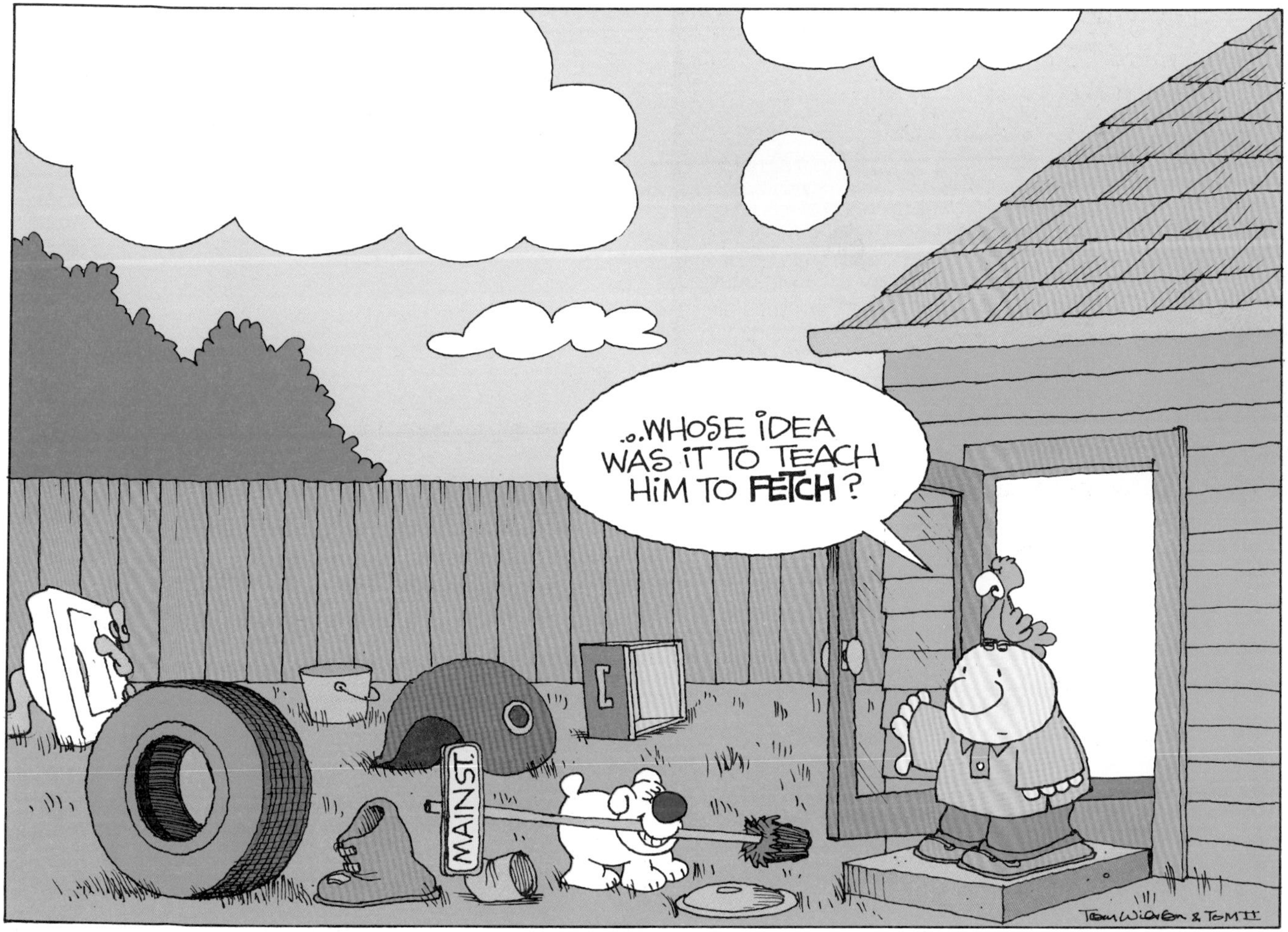
...WHOSE IDEA WAS IT TO TEACH HIM TO FETCH?
MAIN ST.
Tom Wilson & Tom II

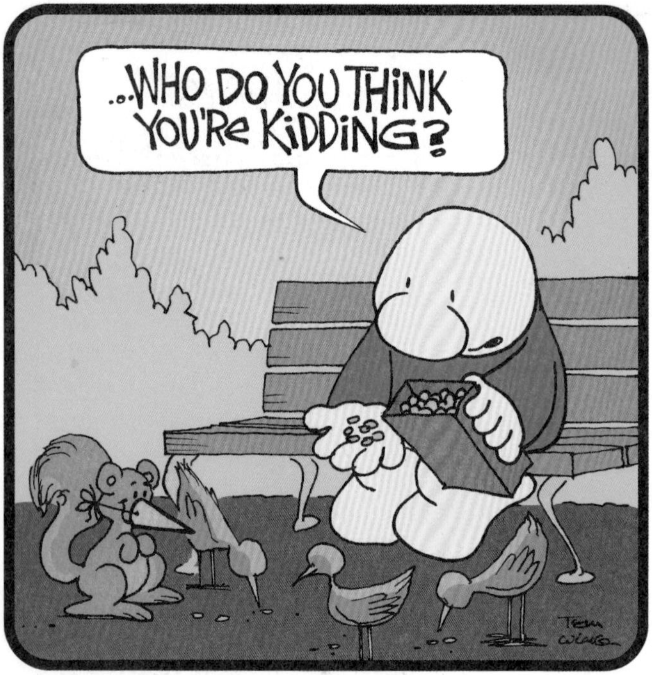
...WHO DO YOU THINK YOU'RE KIDDING?

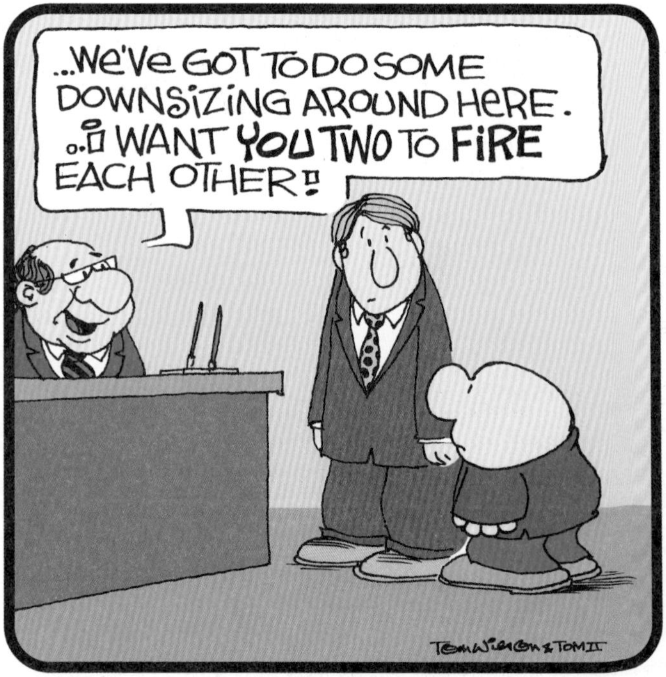
...WE'VE GOT TO DO SOME DOWNSIZING AROUND HERE. ..I WANT YOU TWO TO FIRE EACH OTHER!

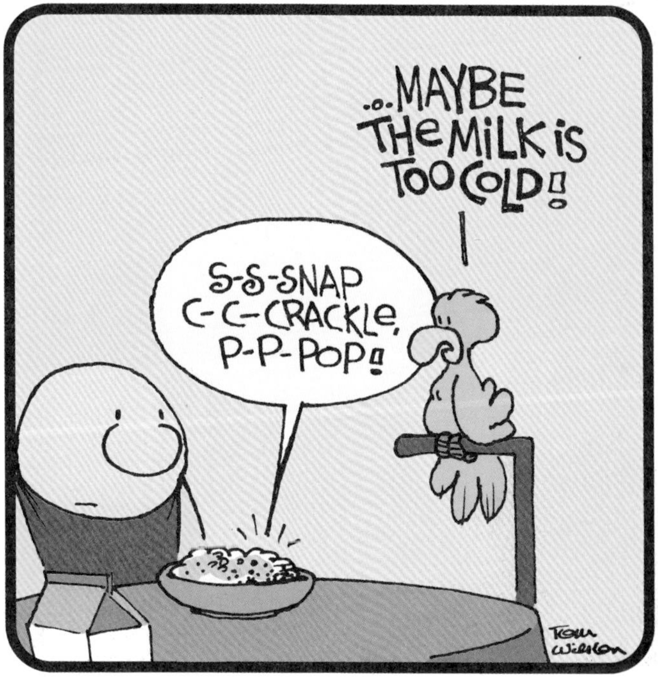
S-S-SNAP
C-C-CRACKLE,
P-P-POP!
..o..MAYBE THE MILK IS TOO COLD!
TOM WILSON

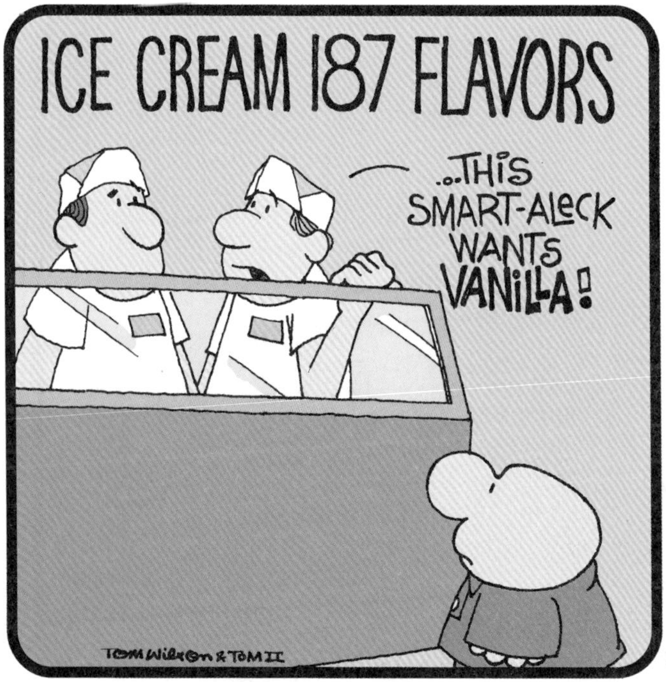
ICE CREAM 187 FLAVORS
..o..THIS SMART-ALECK WANTS VANILLA!
TOM WILSON & TOM II

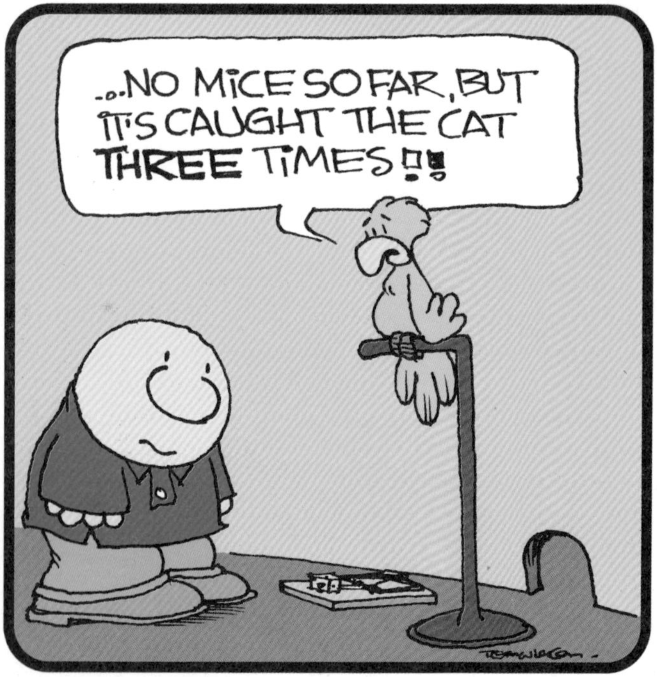
...NO MICE SO FAR, BUT IT'S CAUGHT THE CAT THREE TIMES!!!

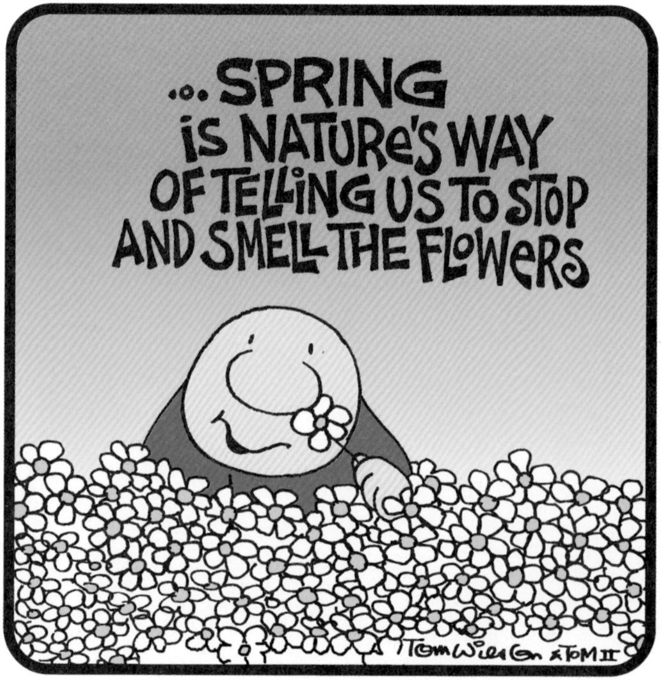
...SPRING IS NATURE'S WAY OF TELLING US TO STOP AND SMELL THE FLOWERS

DETOUR
...ALONG OUR PATH OF LIFE WE GET A SERIES OF DETOURS...
DETOUR
..AND WE ALL GET FRUSTRATED AND IMPATIENT WHEN WE FEEL WE HAVE TO LEAVE THE PATH WE'VE CHOSEN!!
DETOUR
..BUT WHAT IF THE REAL PATH OF LIFE...
DETOUR
...IS REALLY MADE UP OF ALL THESE DETOURS
..AND INSTEAD OF LEARNING THE REAL LESSONS OF LIFE, WE MISS THEM BECAUSE WE WERE TOO BUSY BEING FRUSTRATED & IMPATIENT!!

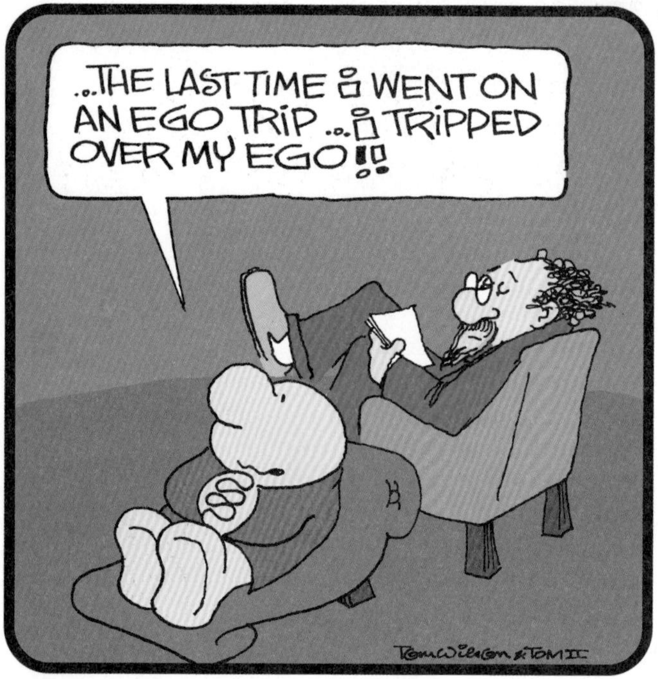
..THE LAST TIME I WENT ON AN EGO TRIP ..I TRIPPED OVER MY EGO!!

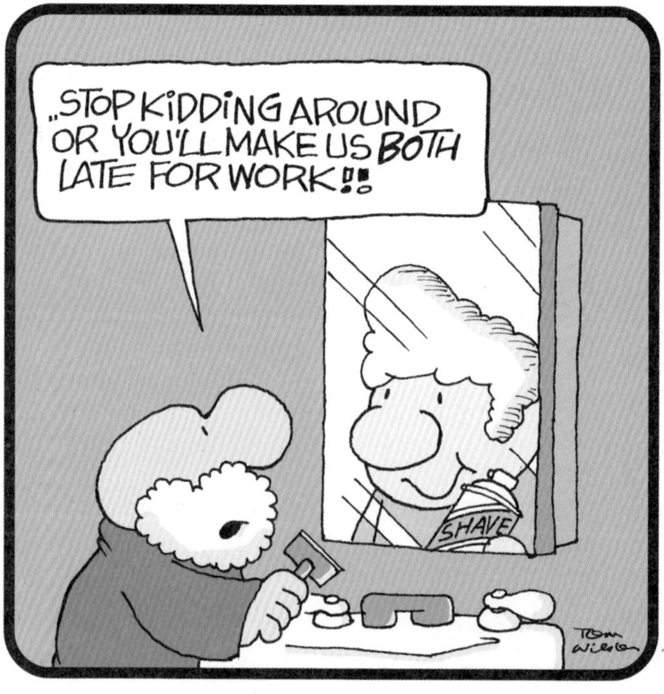
..STOP KIDDING AROUND OR YOU'LL MAKE US BOTH LATE FOR WORK!!
SHAVE

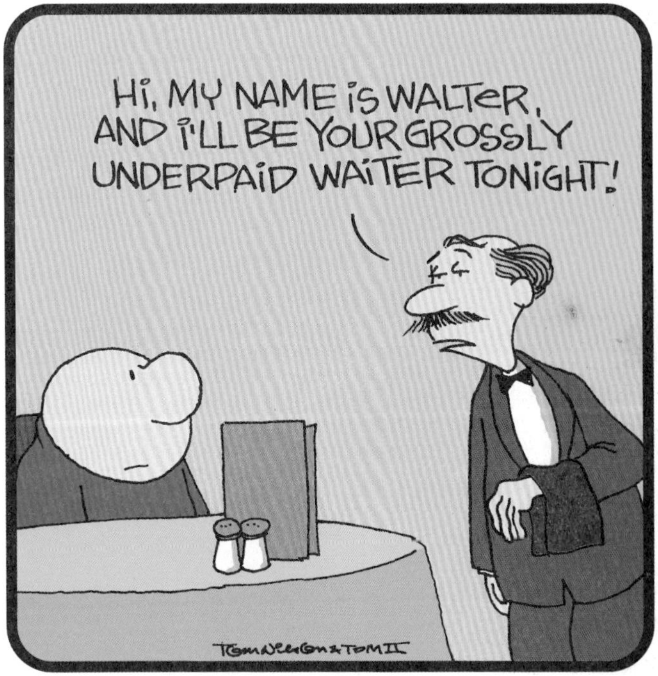
HI, MY NAME IS WALTER, AND I'LL BE YOUR GROSSLY UNDERPAID WAITER TONIGHT!

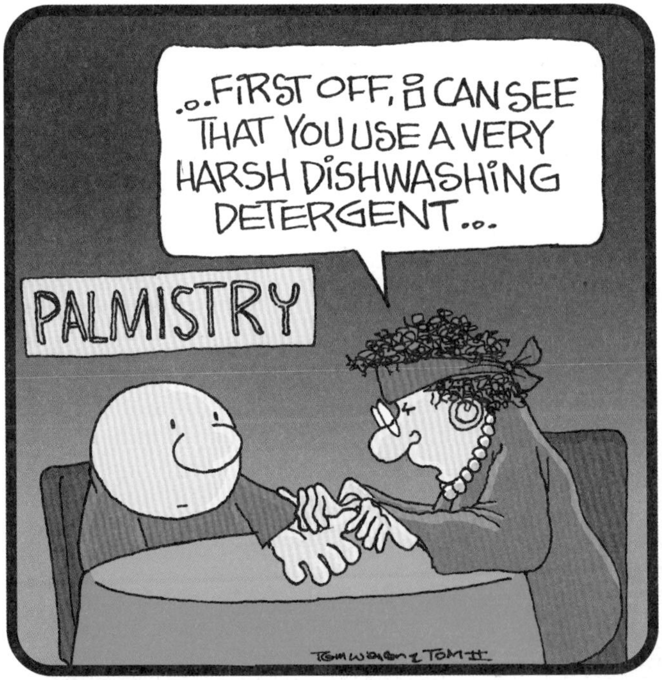
...FIRST OFF, I CAN SEE THAT YOU USE A VERY HARSH DISHWASHING DETERGENT...
PALMISTRY

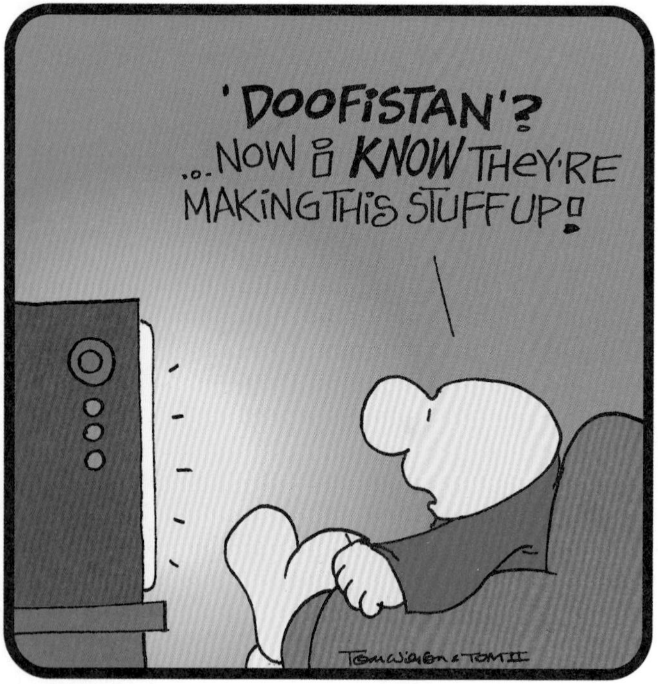
'DOOFISTAN'?
..NOW I KNOW THEY'RE MAKING THIS STUFF UP!
TOM WILSON & TOM II

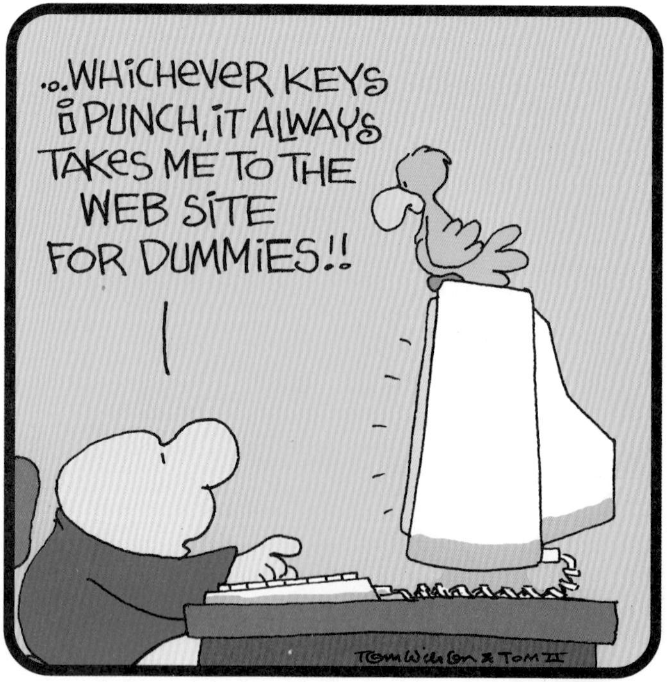
..WHICHEVER KEYS I PUNCH, IT ALWAYS TAKES ME TO THE WEB SITE FOR DUMMIES!!
TOM WILSON & TOM II

EXPECT
THE
UNEXPECTED
EXPECT
THE
UNEXPECTED
?
THUNK
TomWilson & Tom II

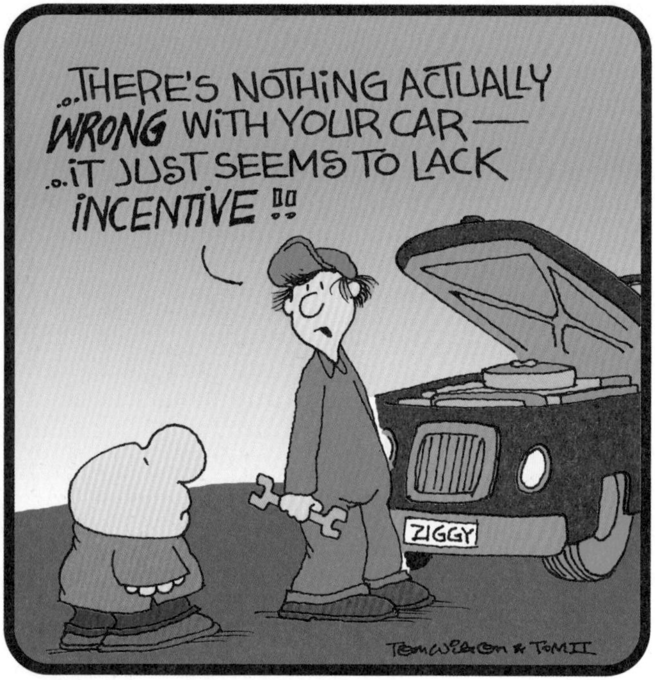

..THERE'S NOTHING ACTUALLY WRONG WITH YOUR CAR— ..iT JUST SEEMS TO LACK iNCENTIVE !!
ZIGGY
TOM WILSON & TOM II

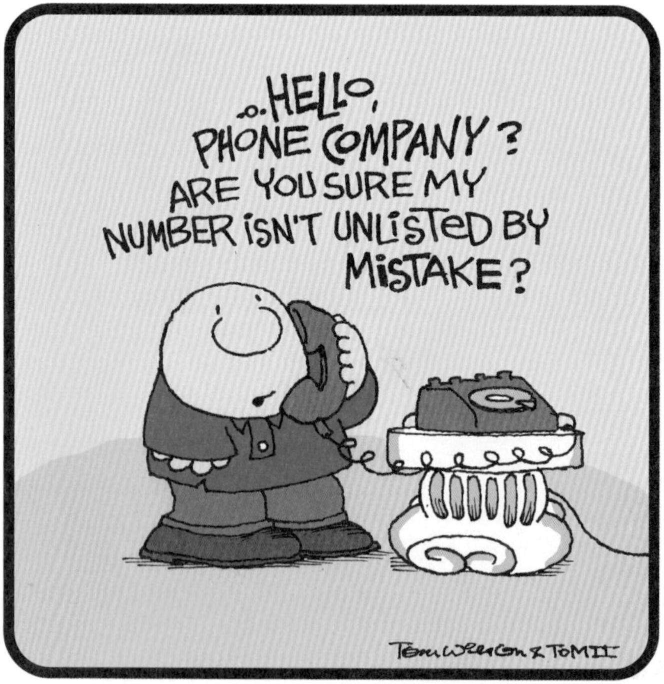

..HELLO, PHONE COMPANY? ARE YOU SURE MY NUMBER iSN'T UNLISTED BY MISTAKE?
TOM WILSON & TOM II

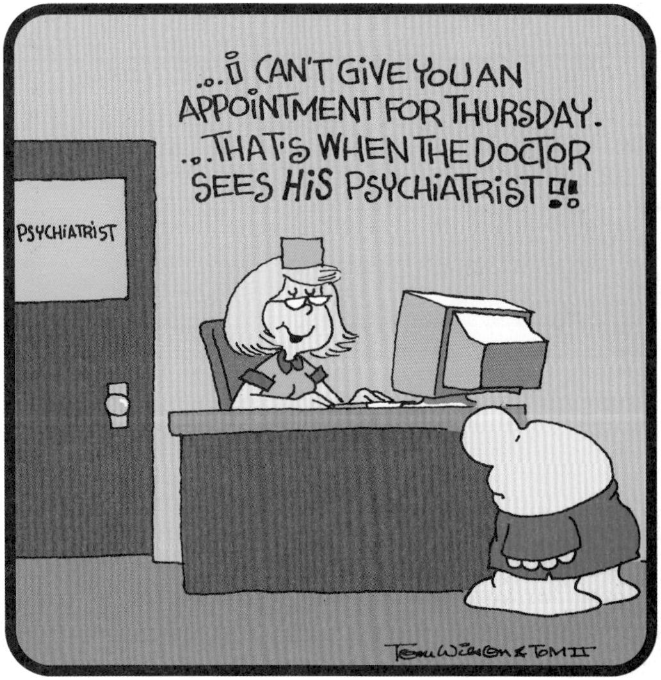
..i CAN'T GIVE YOU AN APPOINTMENT FOR THURSDAY. ..THAT'S WHEN THE DOCTOR SEES HIS PSYCHIATRIST!!
PSYCHIATRIST
Tom Wilson & Tom II

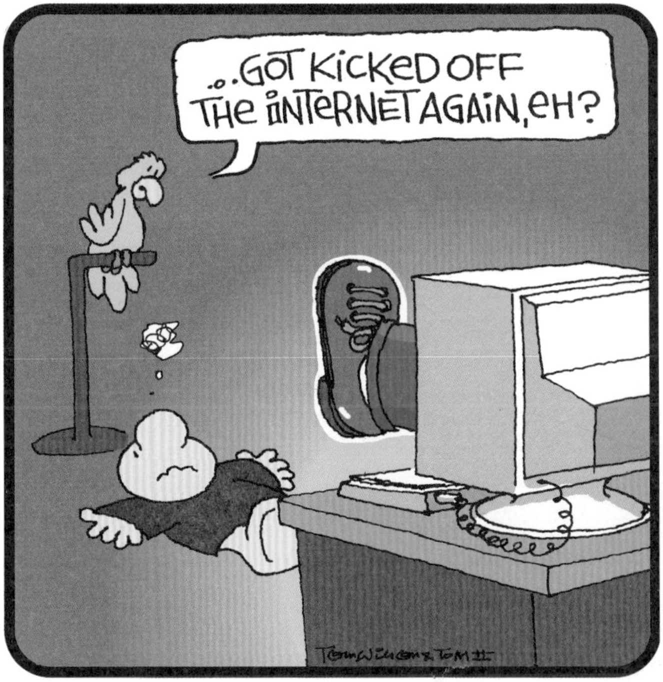
..GOT KICKED OFF THE INTERNET AGAIN, EH?
Tom Wilson & Tom II

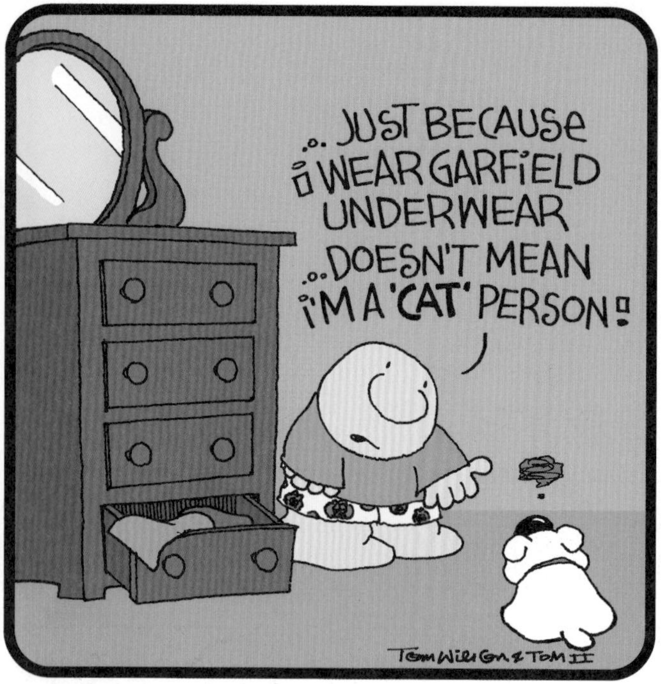
...JUST BECAUSE I WEAR GARFIELD UNDERWEAR ...DOESN'T MEAN I'M A 'CAT' PERSON!
Tom Wilson & Tom II

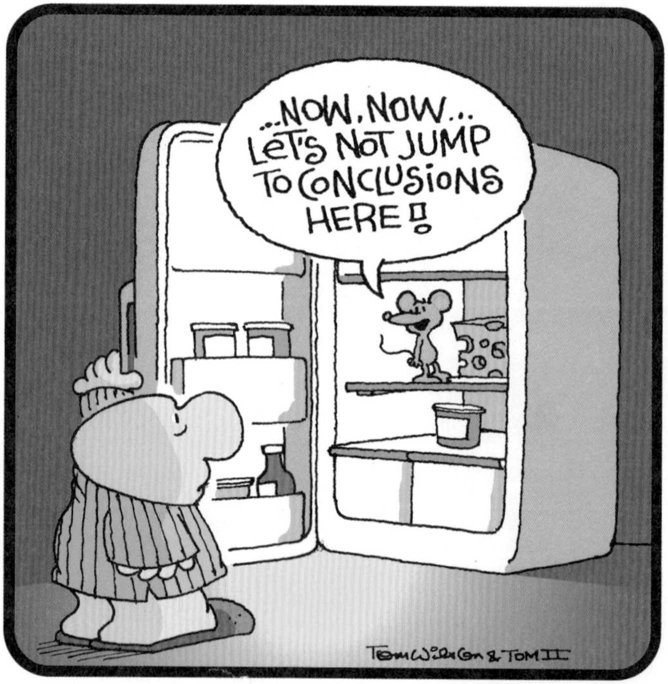
...NOW, NOW... LET'S NOT JUMP TO CONCLUSIONS HERE!
Tom Wilson & Tom II

THE FIRST AND MOST IMPORTANT RULE OF HOME REPAIR IS ALWAYS USE THE RIGHT TOOL FOR THE JOB!!
HOME REPAIR
WHEN ADJUSTING 3-INCH PIPE, THE RIGHT TOOL IS AN ADJUSTABLE 8-INCH CRESCENT WRENCH!
?
?
HELLO?
...FOR ME, THIS IS USUALLY THE RIGHT TOOL FOR EVERY JOB!!
ACME PLUMBING ..MAY I HELP YOU?

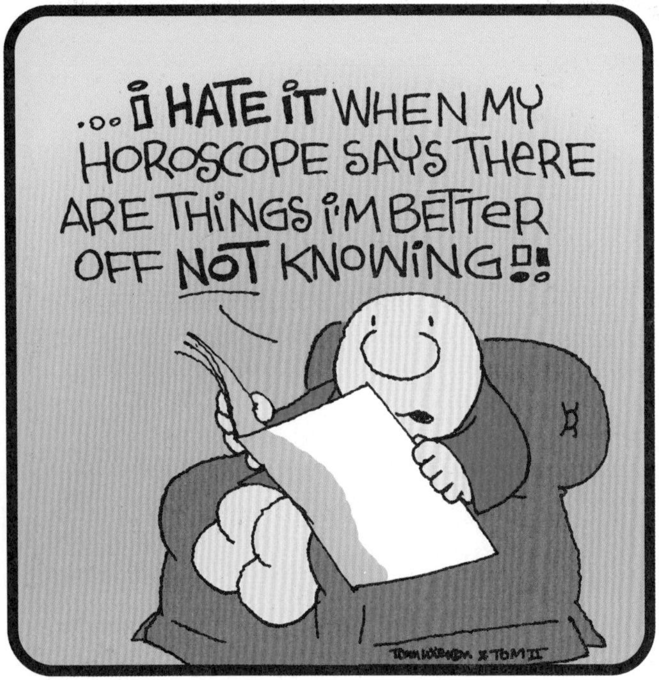
...I HATE IT WHEN MY HOROSCOPE SAYS THERE ARE THINGS I'M BETTER OFF NOT KNOWING!!

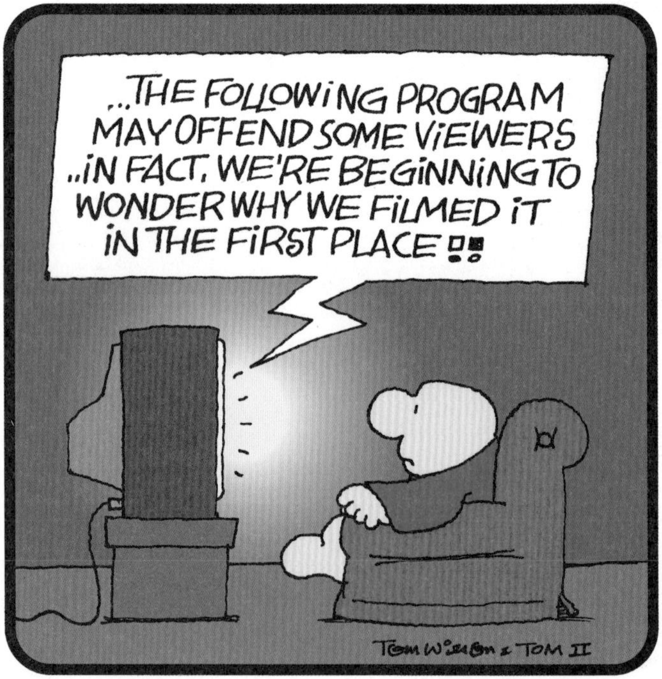
...THE FOLLOWING PROGRAM MAY OFFEND SOME VIEWERS ..IN FACT, WE'RE BEGINNING TO WONDER WHY WE FILMED IT IN THE FIRST PLACE!!
TOM WILSON & TOM II

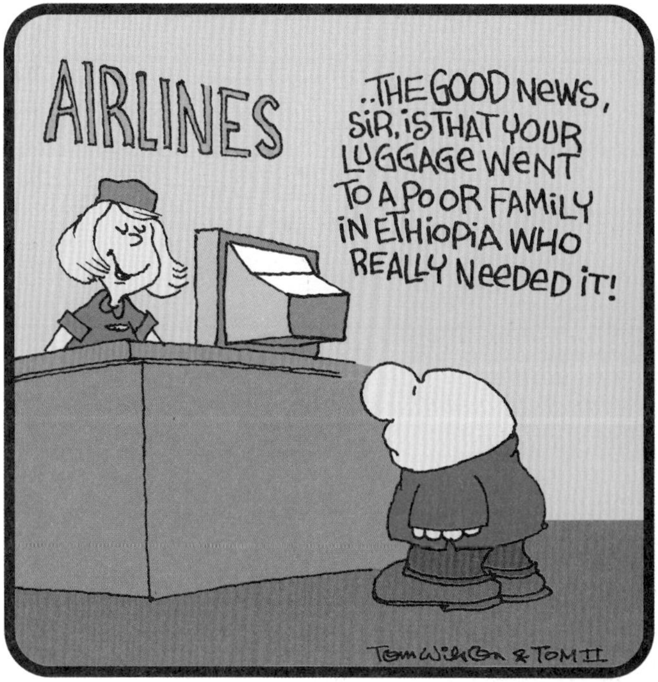
AIRLINES
..THE GOOD NEWS, SIR, IS THAT YOUR LUGGAGE WENT TO A POOR FAMILY IN ETHIOPIA WHO REALLY NEEDED IT!
Tom Wilson & TOM II

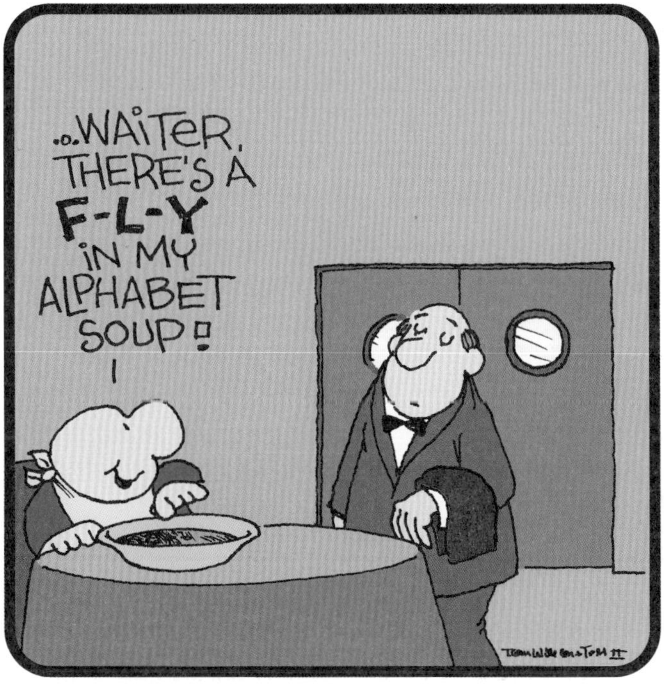
..WAITER, THERE'S A F-L-Y IN MY ALPHABET SOUP!!

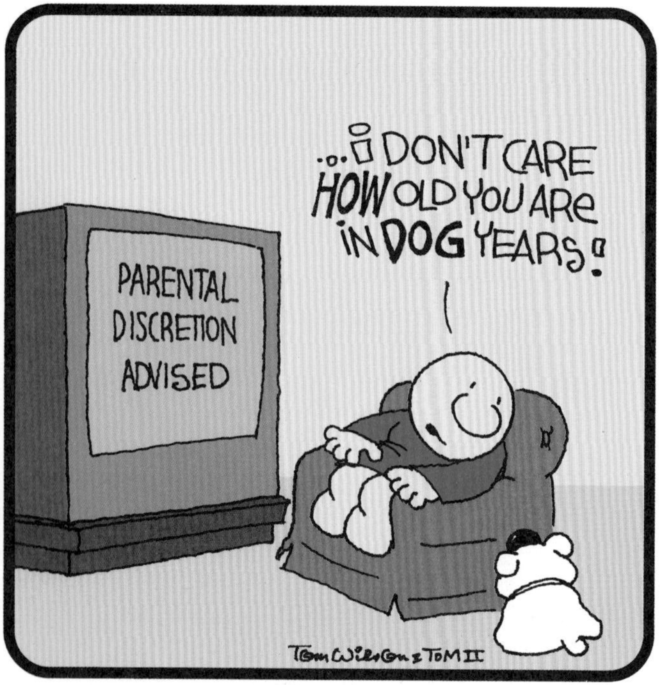
...I DON'T CARE HOW OLD YOU ARE IN DOG YEARS!
PARENTAL DISCRETION ADVISED
TOM WILSON & TOM II

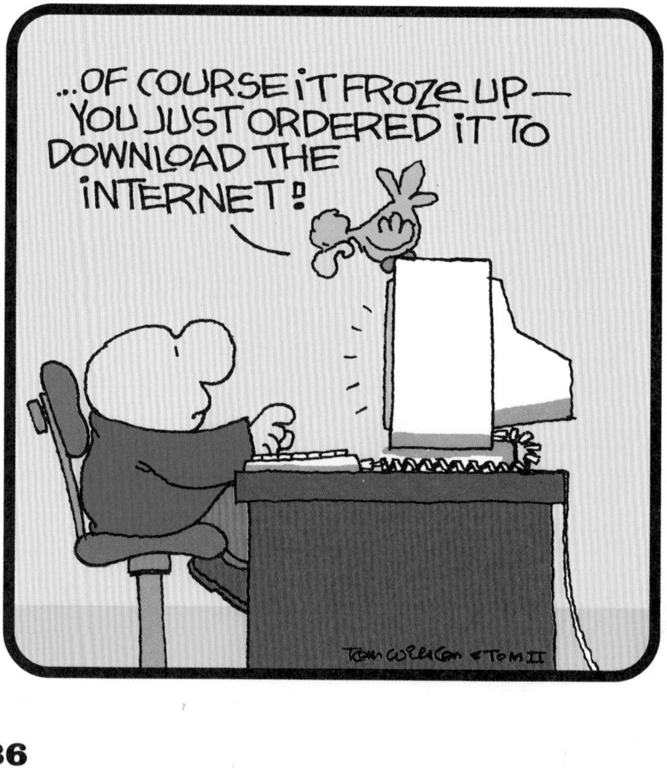
...OF COURSE IT FROZE UP— YOU JUST ORDERED IT TO DOWNLOAD THE INTERNET!
TOM WILSON & TOM II

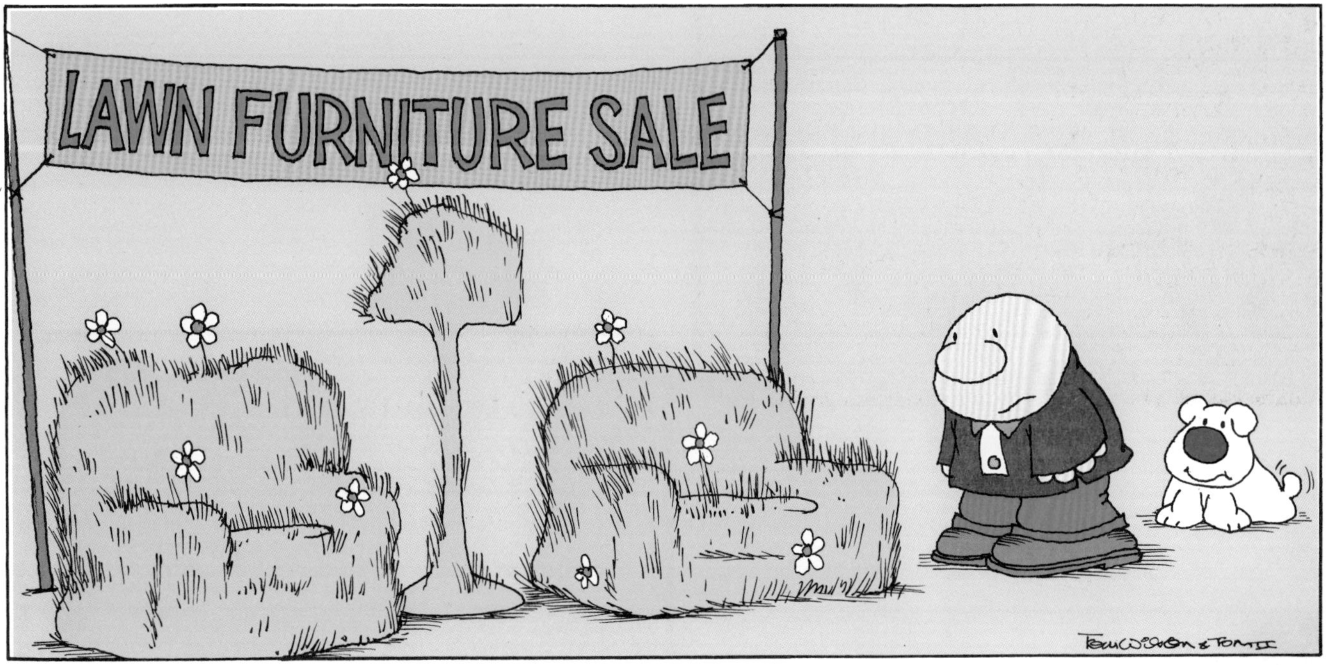
LAWN FURNITURE SALE

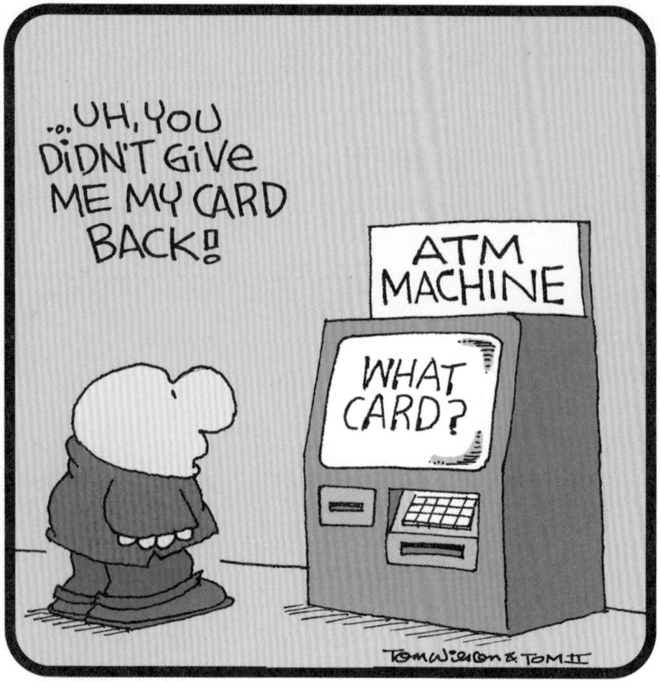
..UH, YOU DIDN'T GIVE ME MY CARD BACK!
ATM MACHINE
WHAT CARD?
TOM WILSON & TOM II

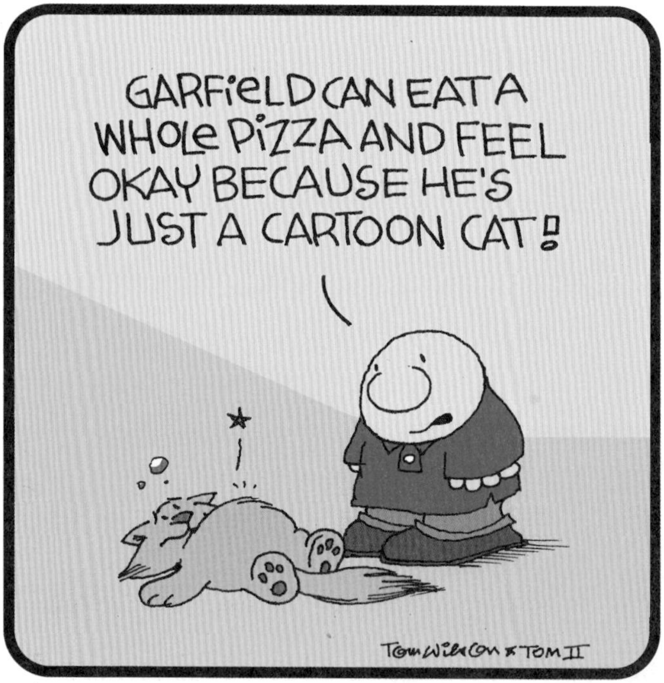
GARFIELD CAN EAT A WHOLE PIZZA AND FEEL OKAY BECAUSE HE'S JUST A CARTOON CAT!
TOM WILSON & TOM II

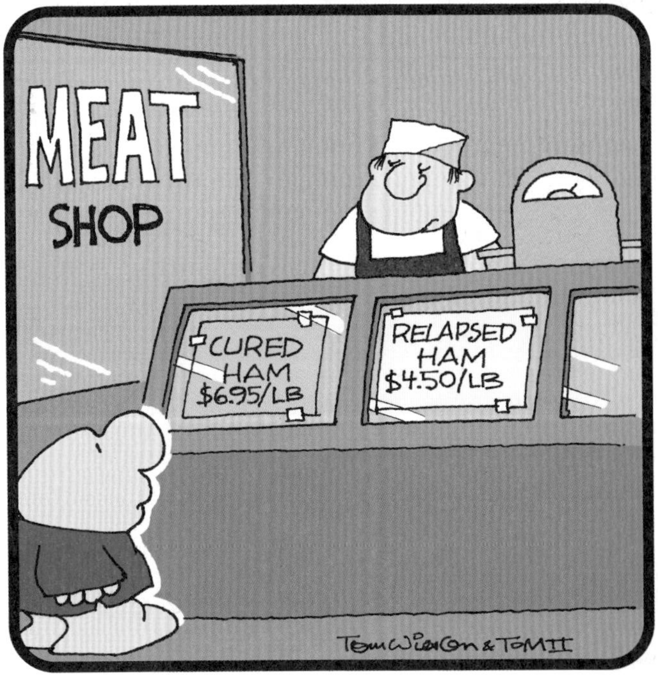
MEAT
SHOP
CURED HAM $6.95/LB
RELAPSED HAM $4.50/LB
Tom Wilson & Tom II

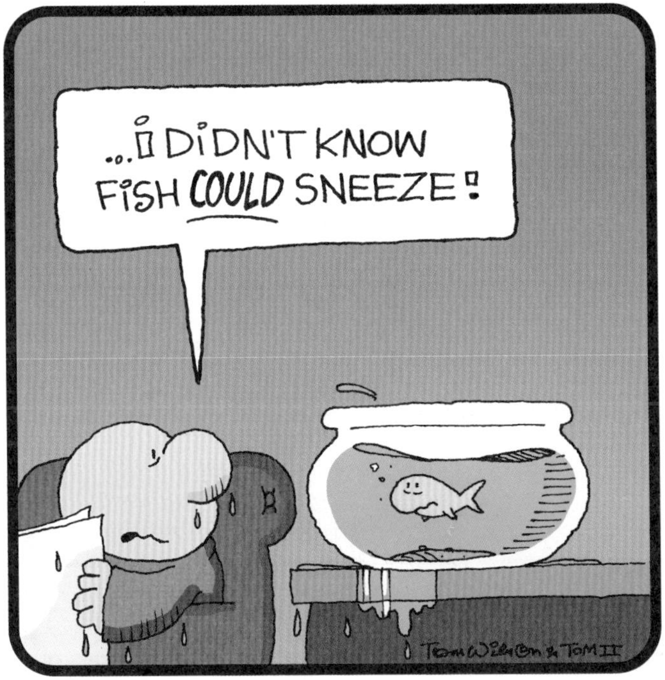
...I DIDN'T KNOW FISH COULD SNEEZE!
Tom Wilson & Tom II

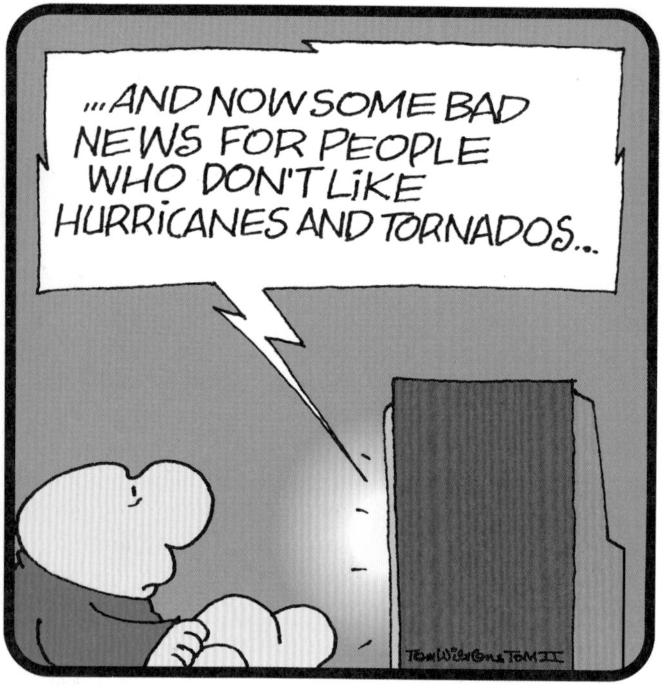
...AND NOW SOME BAD NEWS FOR PEOPLE WHO DON'T LIKE HURRICANES AND TORNADOS...
TOM WILSON & TOM II

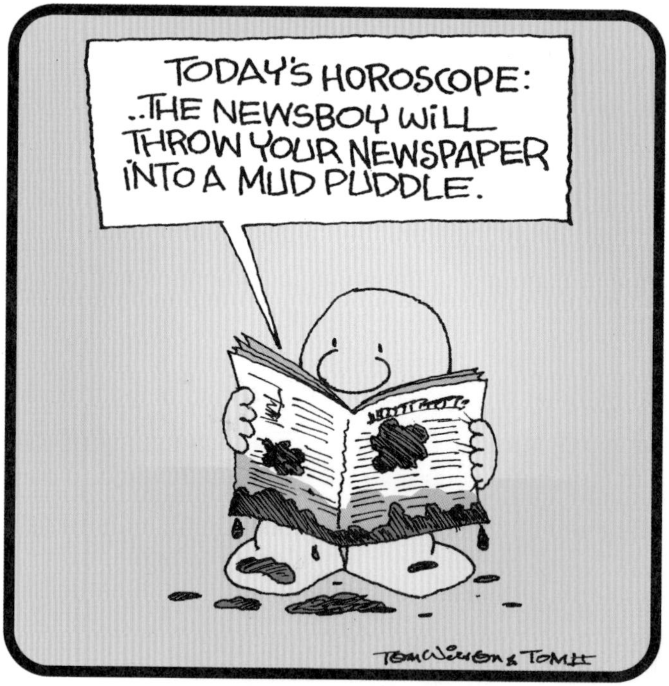
TODAY'S HOROSCOPE: ..THE NEWSBOY WILL THROW YOUR NEWSPAPER INTO A MUD PUDDLE.
TOM WILSON & TOM II

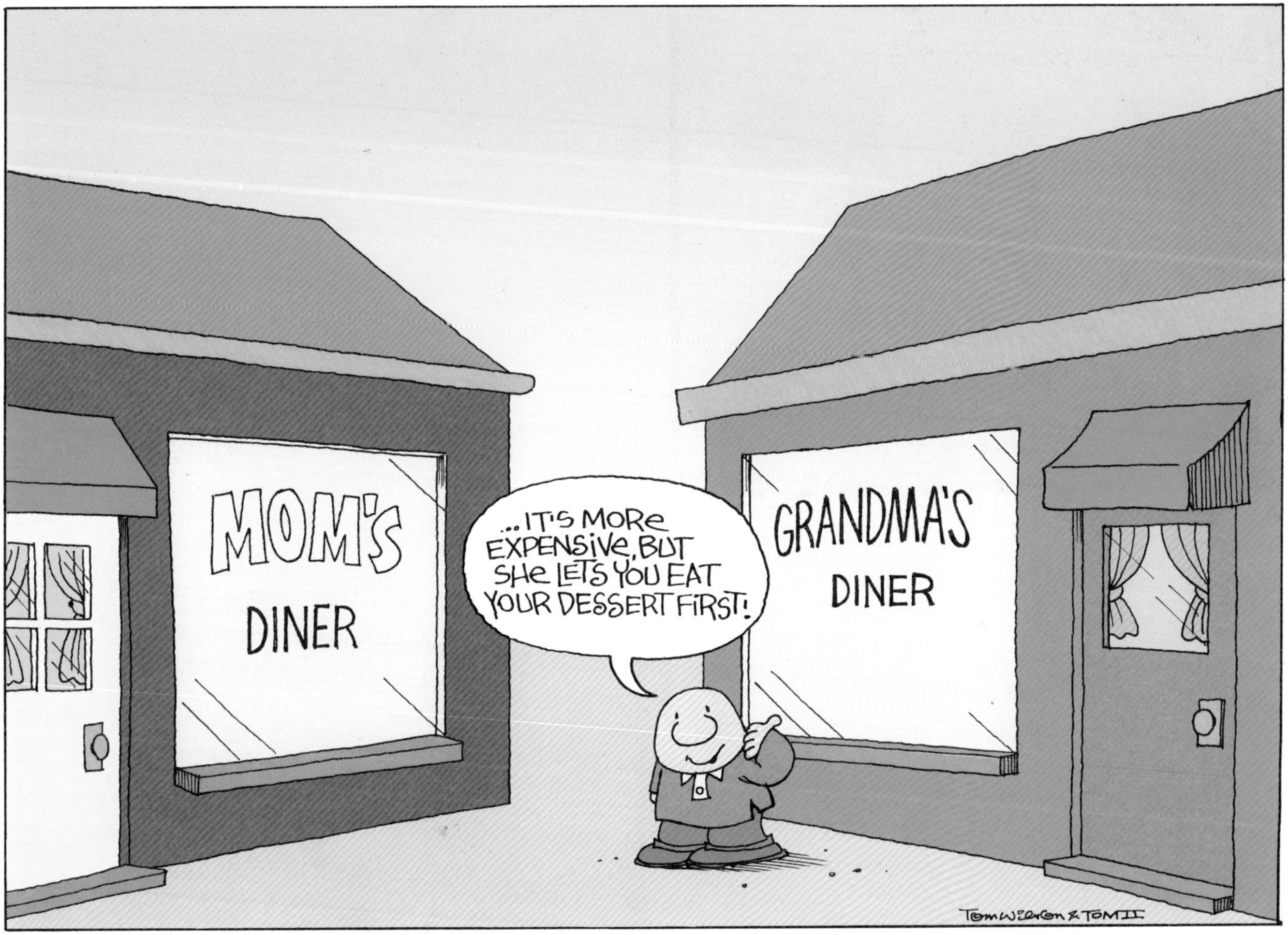
MOM'S
DINER
...IT'S MORE EXPENSIVE, BUT SHE LETS YOU EAT YOUR DESSERT FIRST!
GRANDMA'S
DINER

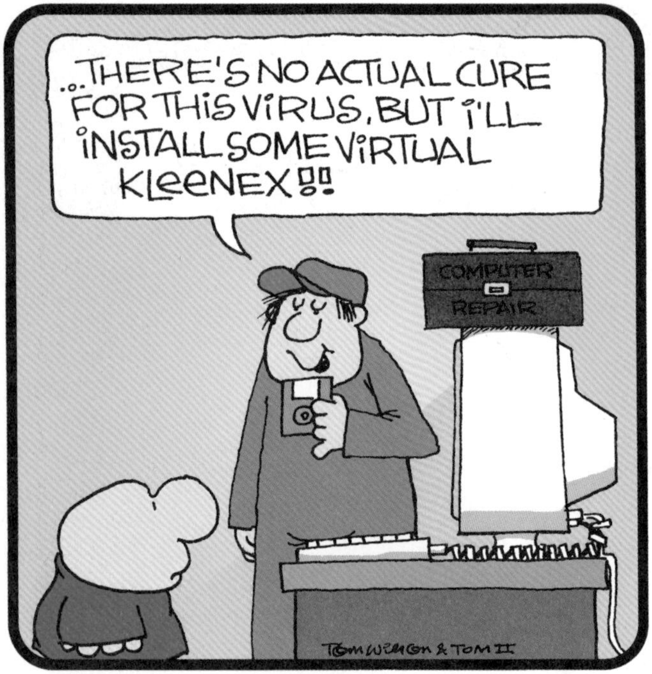
..THERE'S NO ACTUAL CURE FOR THIS VIRUS, BUT I'LL INSTALL SOME VIRTUAL KLEENEX!!
COMPUTER REPAIR

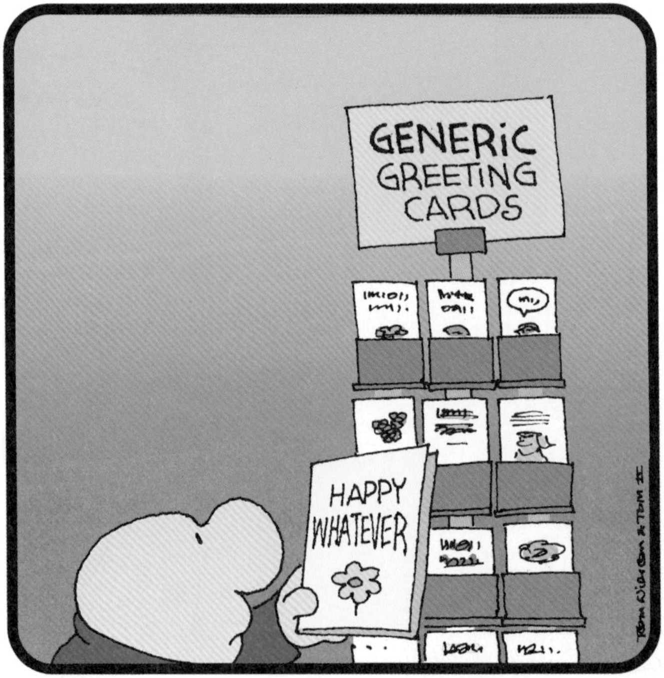
GENERIC GREETING CARDS
HAPPY WHATEVER

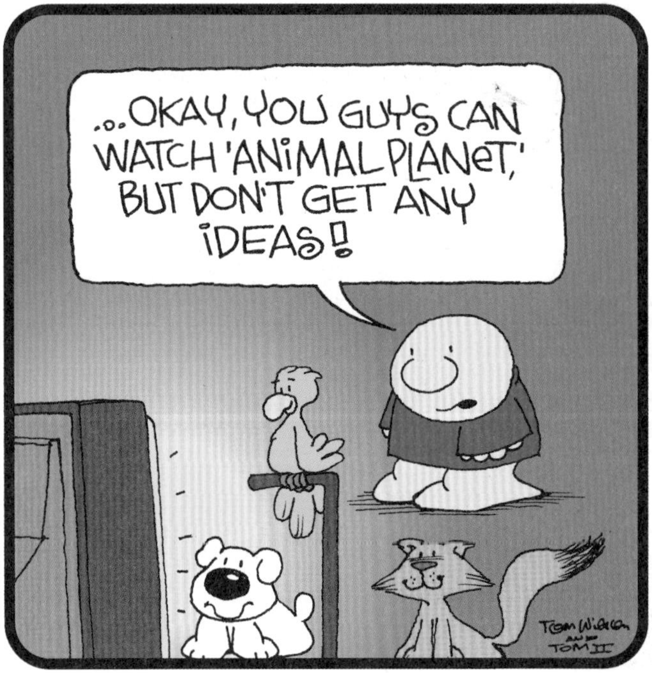
...OKAY, YOU GUYS CAN WATCH 'ANIMAL PLANET,' BUT DON'T GET ANY IDEAS!
Tom Wilson and Tom II

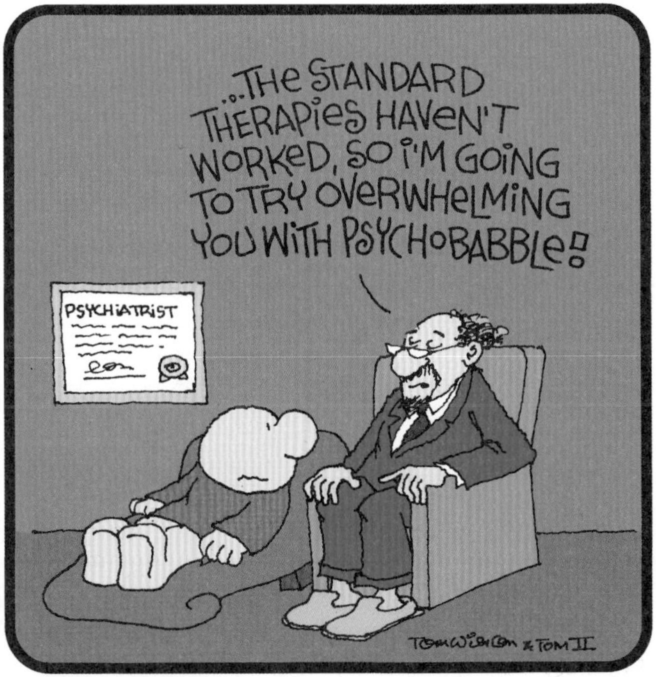
...THE STANDARD THERAPIES HAVEN'T WORKED, SO I'M GOING TO TRY OVERWHELMING YOU WITH PSYCHOBABBLE!
PSYCHIATRIST
Tom Wilson & Tom II

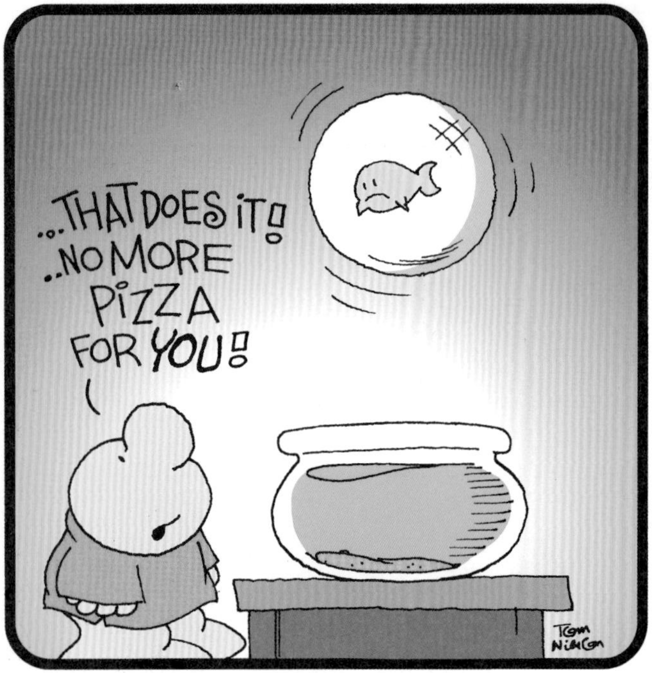
..THAT DOES IT!
..NO MORE PIZZA FOR YOU!
TOM WILSON

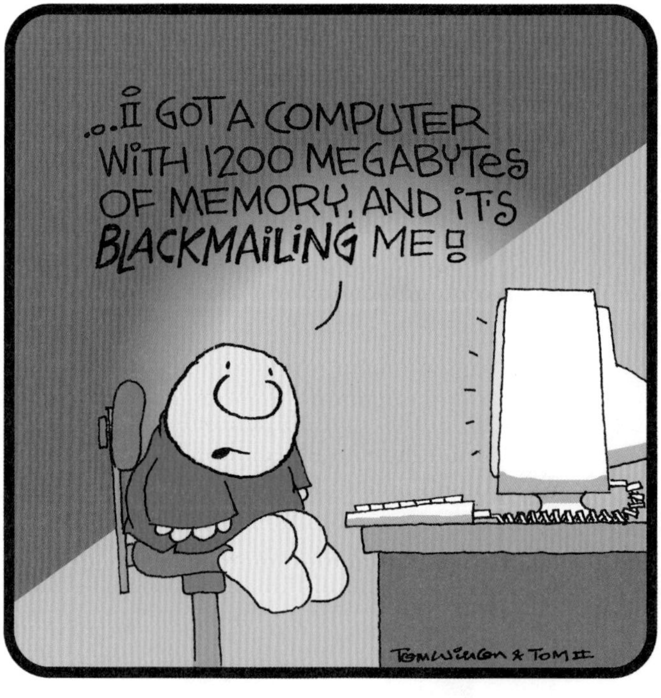
..I GOT A COMPUTER WITH 1200 MEGABYTES OF MEMORY, AND IT'S BLACKMAILING ME!
TOM WILSON & TOM II

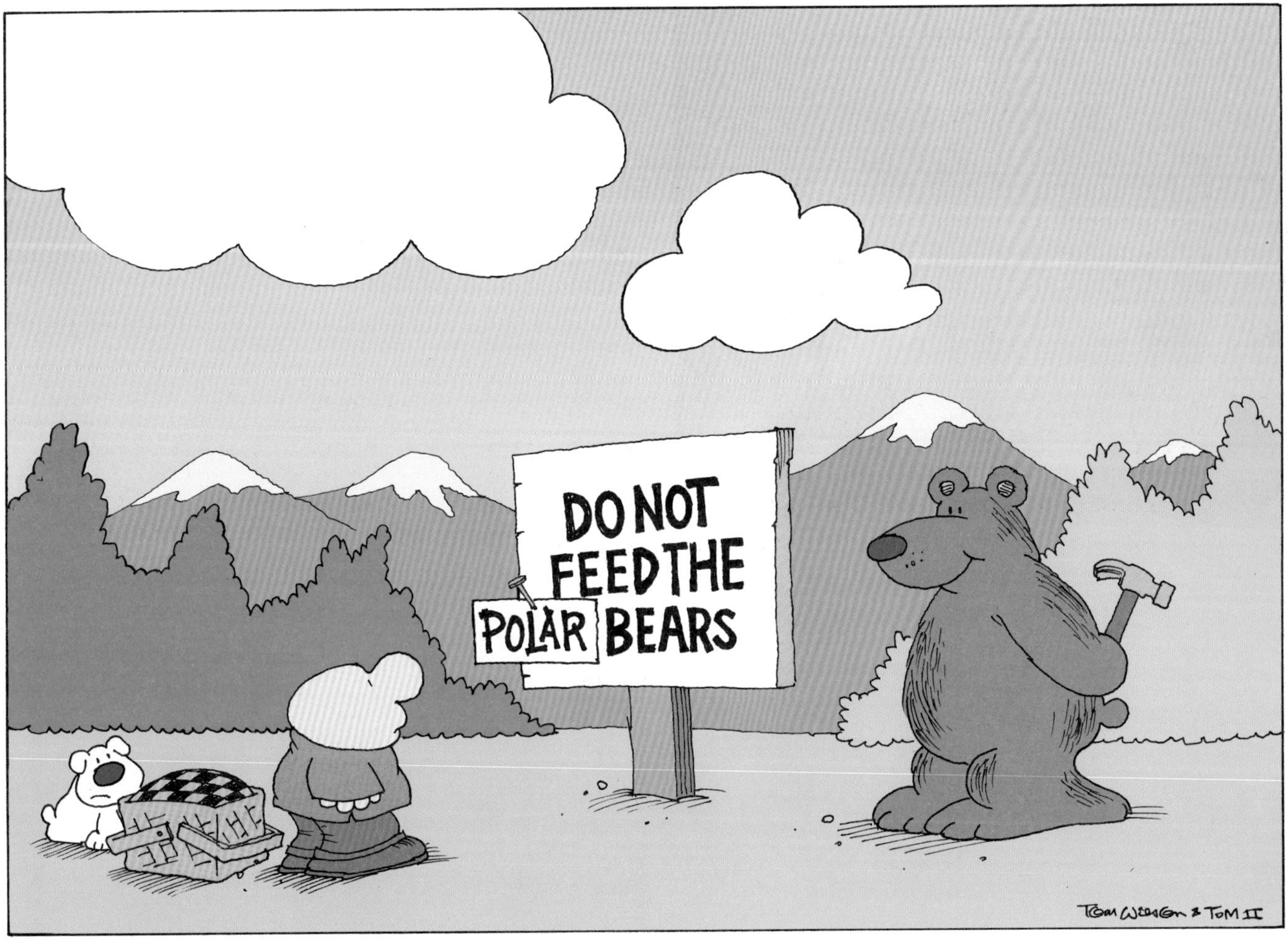
DO NOT
FEED THE
POLAR BEARS
TOM WILSON & TOM II

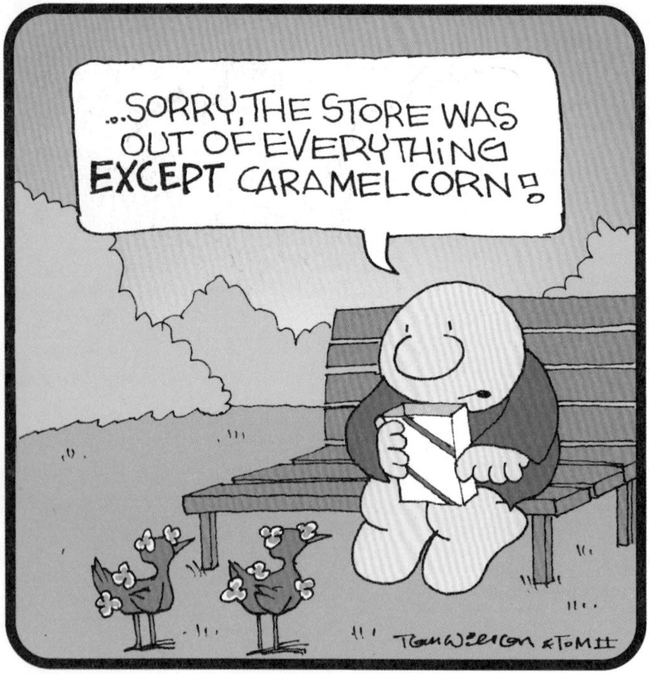
..SORRY, THE STORE WAS OUT OF EVERYTHING EXCEPT CARAMEL CORN!!
Tom Wilson & Tom II

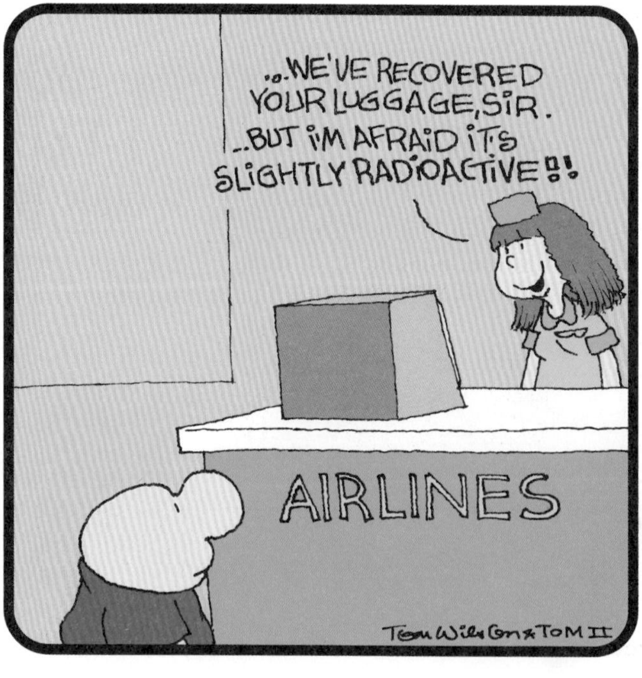
..WE'VE RECOVERED YOUR LUGGAGE, SIR. ..BUT I'M AFRAID IT'S SLIGHTLY RADIOACTIVE!!
AIRLINES
Tom Wilson & Tom II

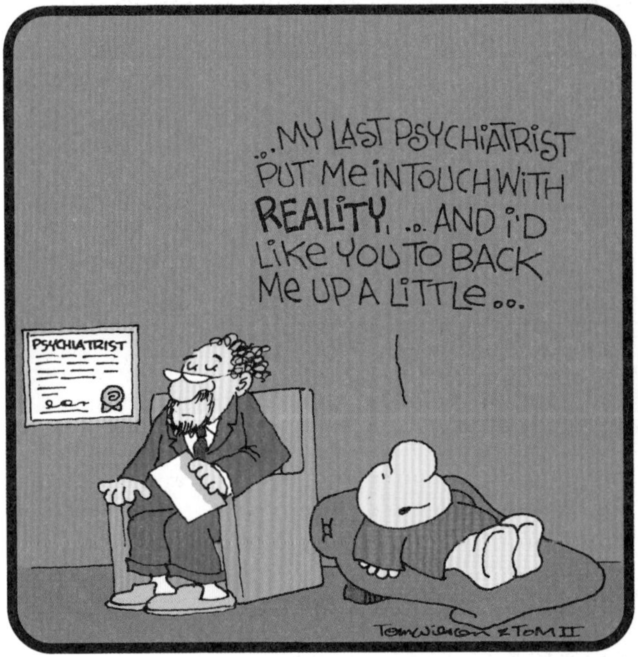
...MY LAST PSYCHIATRIST PUT ME IN TOUCH WITH REALITY. ...AND I'D LIKE YOU TO BACK ME UP A LITTLE...
PSYCHIATRIST

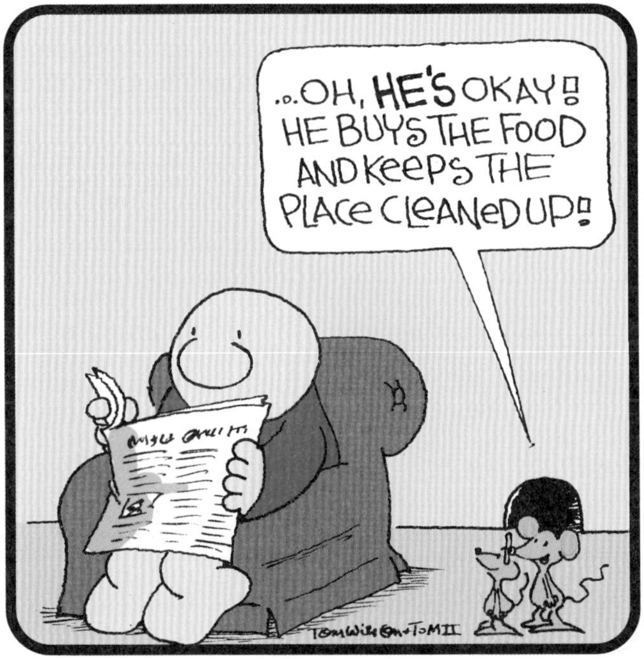
...OH, HE'S OKAY! HE BUYS THE FOOD AND KEEPS THE PLACE CLEANED UP!

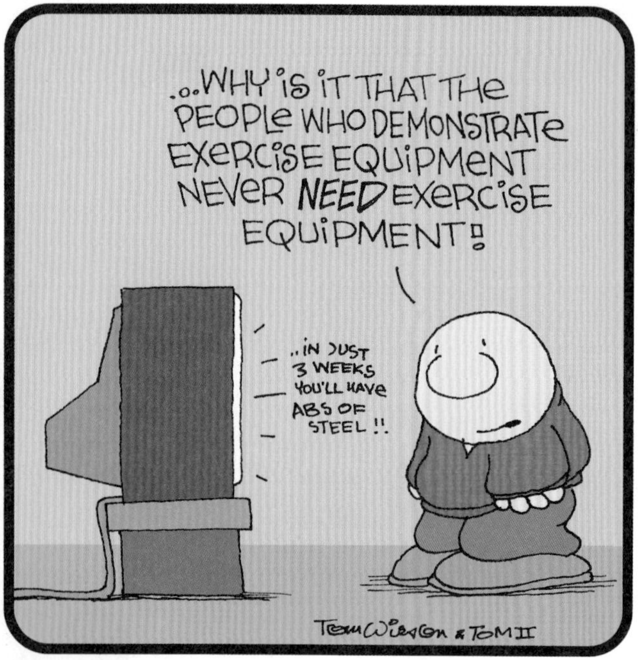
..WHY IS IT THAT THE PEOPLE WHO DEMONSTRATE EXERCISE EQUIPMENT NEVER **NEED** EXERCISE EQUIPMENT!!
..IN JUST 3 WEEKS YOU'LL HAVE ABS OF STEEL!!
TOM WILSON & TOM II

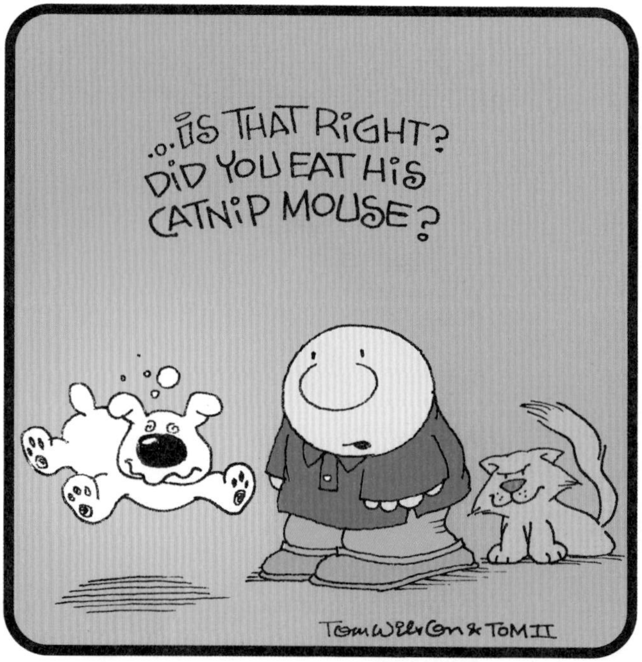
..IS THAT RIGHT? DID YOU EAT HIS CATNIP MOUSE?
TOM WILSON & TOM II

SOMETIMES I THINK THAT IN LIFE'S JOURNEY SOME OF US GET SO LOST..

...BECAUSE DEEP DOWN INSIDE, SOME REALLY LIVE FOR THE SEARCH FOR WHO THEY REALLY ARE!

...AND THE MORE LOST THEY BECOME..

..THE MORE THEY GET TO SEARCH FOR THEIR TRUE SELVES!!

..SO BASICALLY, SOME OF US REALLY NEED TO BE LOST..

..IN ORDER TO FIND OURSELVES!!

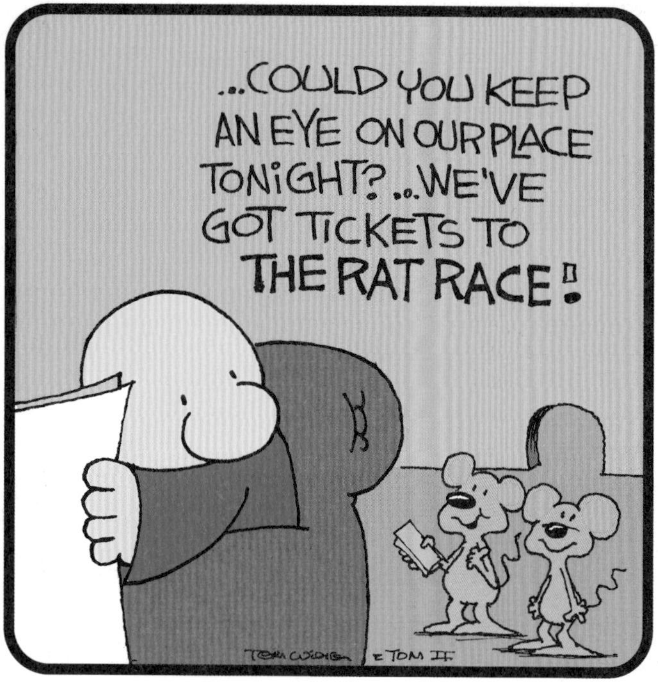
...COULD YOU KEEP AN EYE ON OUR PLACE TONIGHT? ...WE'VE GOT TICKETS TO THE RAT RACE!
TOM WILSON & TOM II

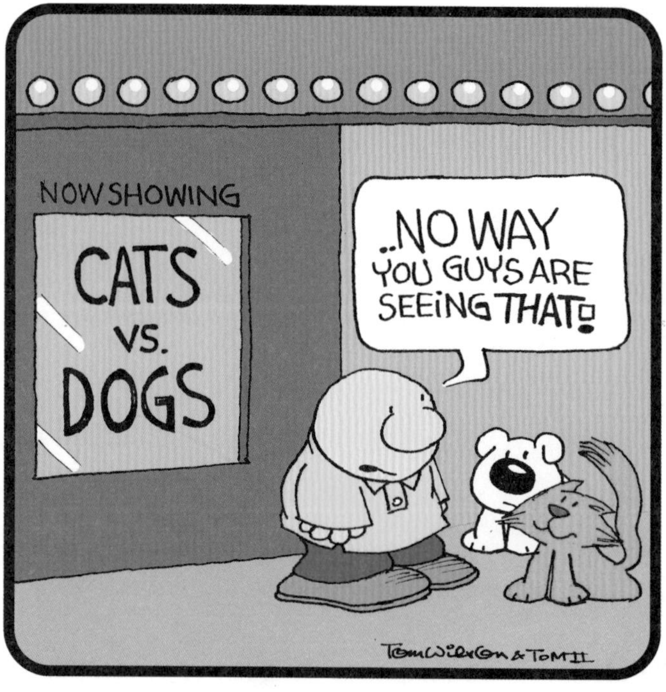
NOW SHOWING
CATS VS. DOGS
..NO WAY YOU GUYS ARE SEEING THAT!
TOM WILSON & TOM II

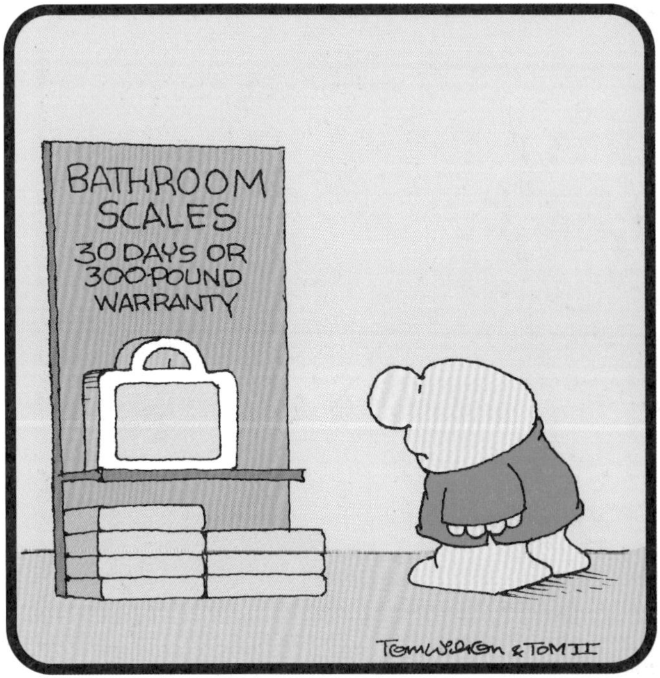
BATHROOM SCALES
30 DAYS OR 300-POUND WARRANTY
TOM WILSON & TOM II

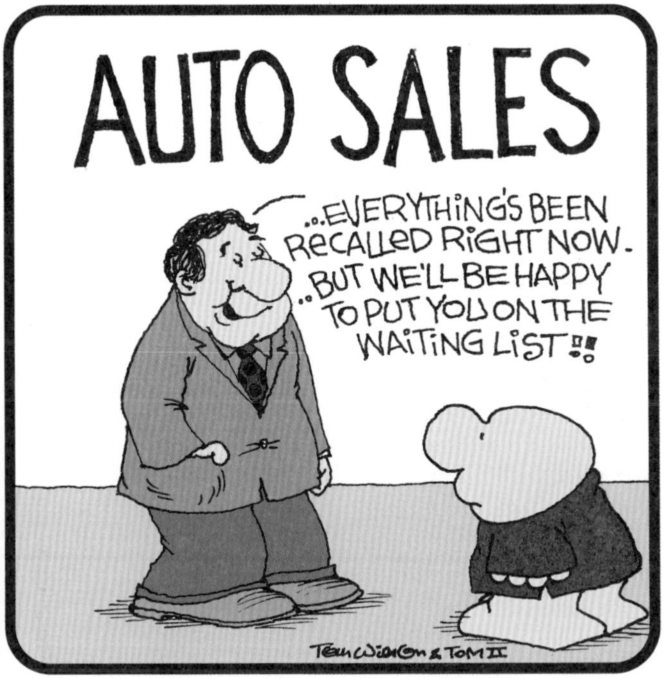
AUTO SALES
..EVERYTHING'S BEEN RECALLED RIGHT NOW. ..BUT WE'LL BE HAPPY TO PUT YOU ON THE WAITING LIST!!
TOM WILSON & TOM II

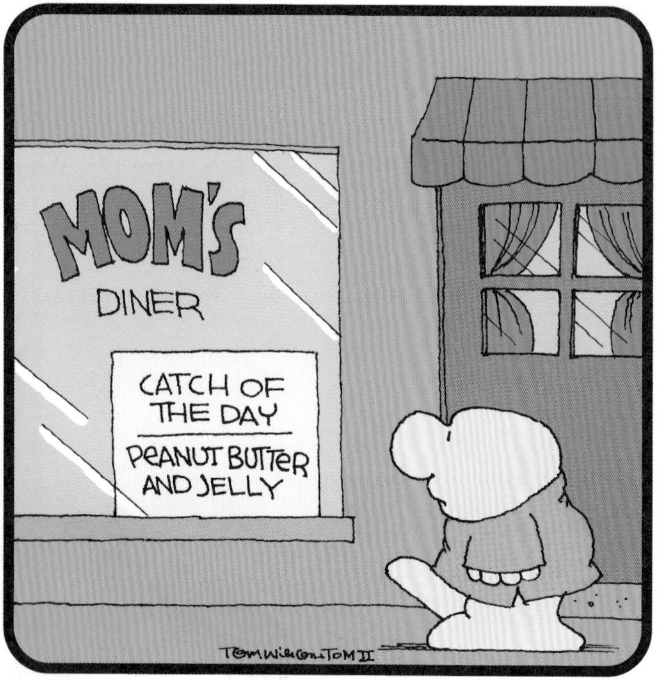
MOM'S
DINER
CATCH OF THE DAY
PEANUT BUTTER AND JELLY
TOM WILSON & TOM II

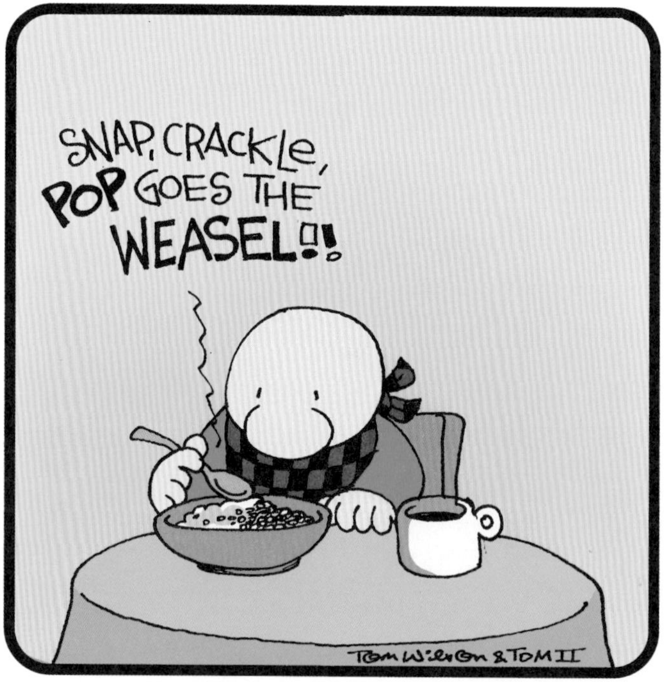
SNAP, CRACKLE, POP GOES THE WEASEL!!!
TOM WILSON & TOM II

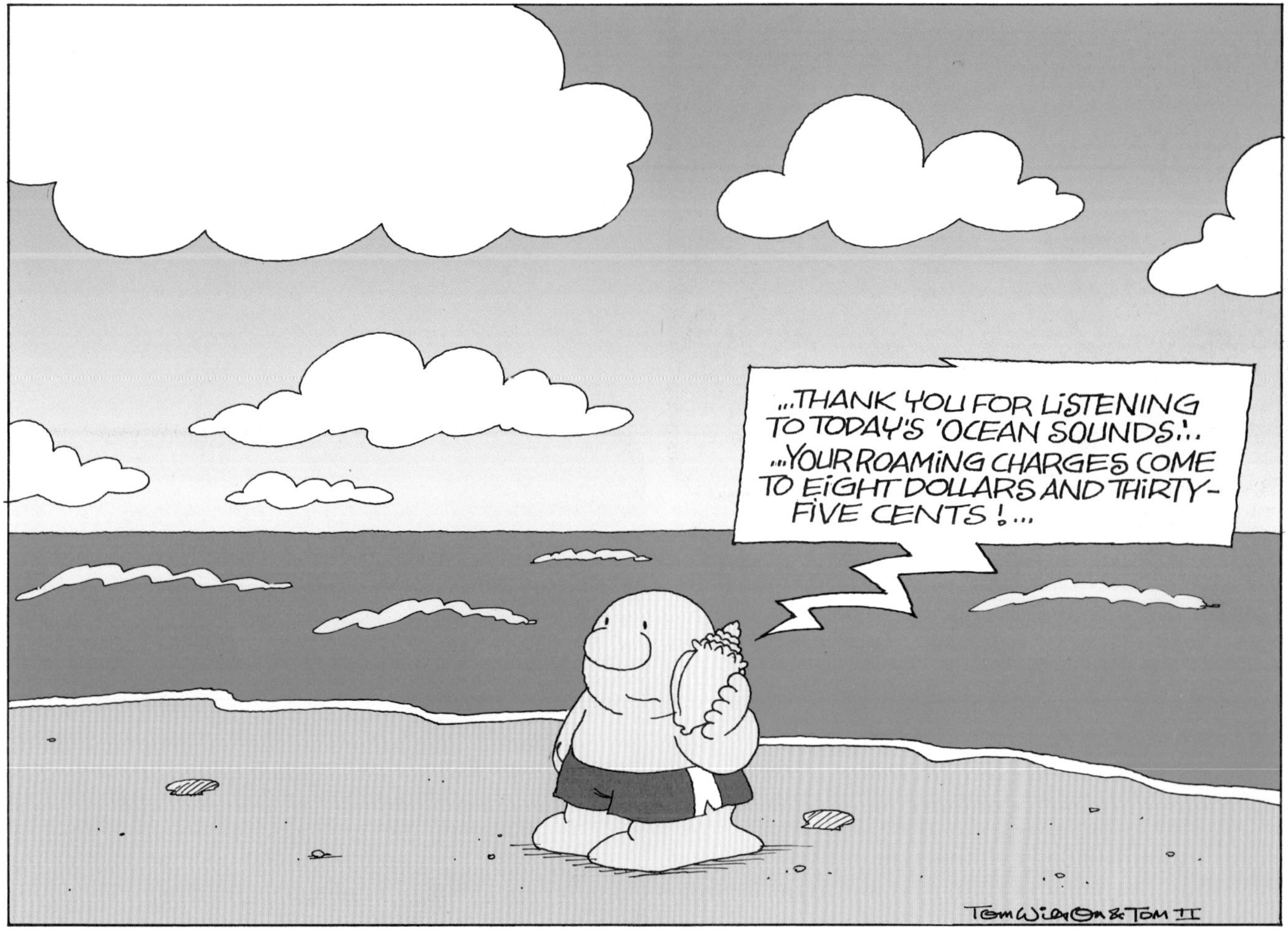
...THANK YOU FOR LISTENING TO TODAY'S 'OCEAN SOUNDS.'... ...YOUR ROAMING CHARGES COME TO EIGHT DOLLARS AND THIRTY-FIVE CENTS!...
TOM WILSON & TOM II

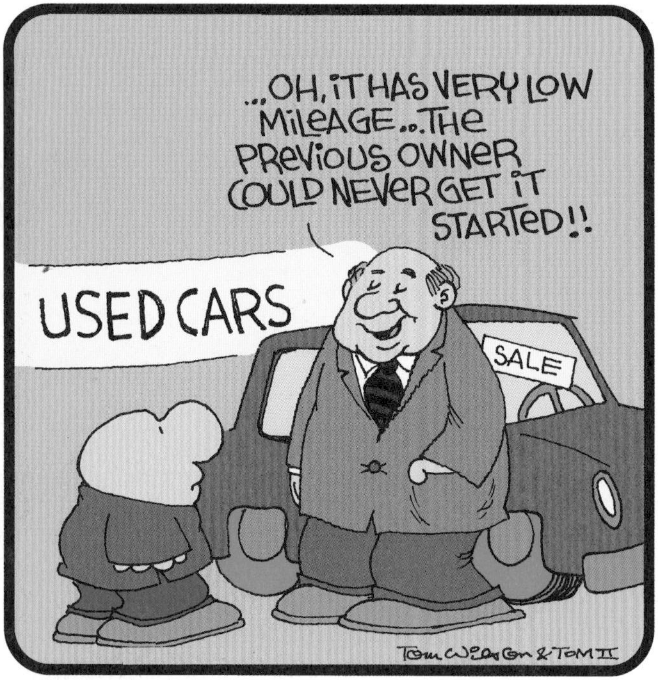
...OH, IT HAS VERY LOW MILEAGE...THE PREVIOUS OWNER COULD NEVER GET IT STARTED!!
USED CARS
SALE
TOM WILSON & TOM II

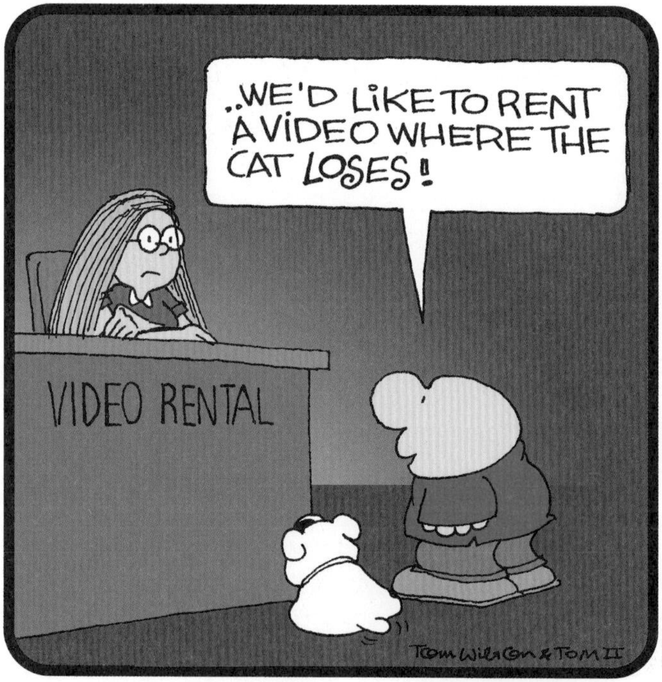
..WE'D LIKE TO RENT A VIDEO WHERE THE CAT LOSES!
VIDEO RENTAL
TOM WILSON & TOM II

...THE DIET PLATE IS THE SAME AS THE REGULAR PLATE, EXCEPT I SIT DOWN AND EAT PART OF IT!
TOM WILSON & TOM II

BLOCKBUSTER
...SOMETHING NICE AND BORING TO FALL ASLEEP IN FRONT OF!!
VIDEOS
TOM WILSON & TOM II

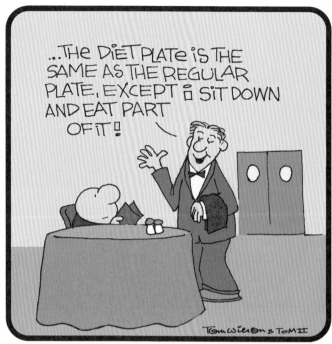

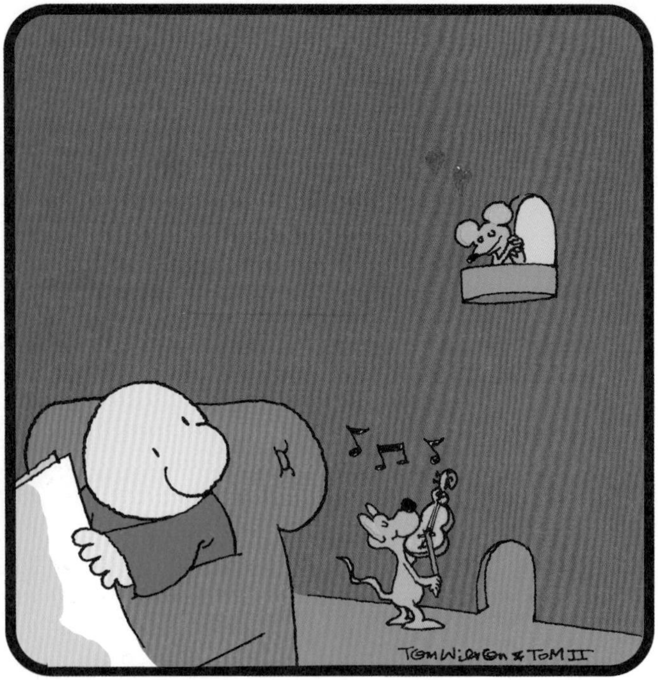
Tom Wilson & Tom II

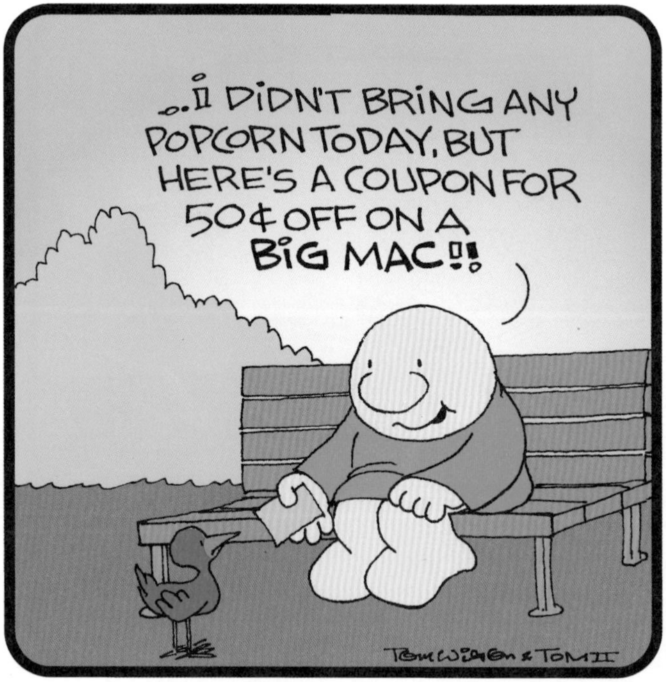
...I DIDN'T BRING ANY POPCORN TODAY, BUT HERE'S A COUPON FOR 50¢ OFF ON A BIG MAC!!
Tom Wilson & Tom II

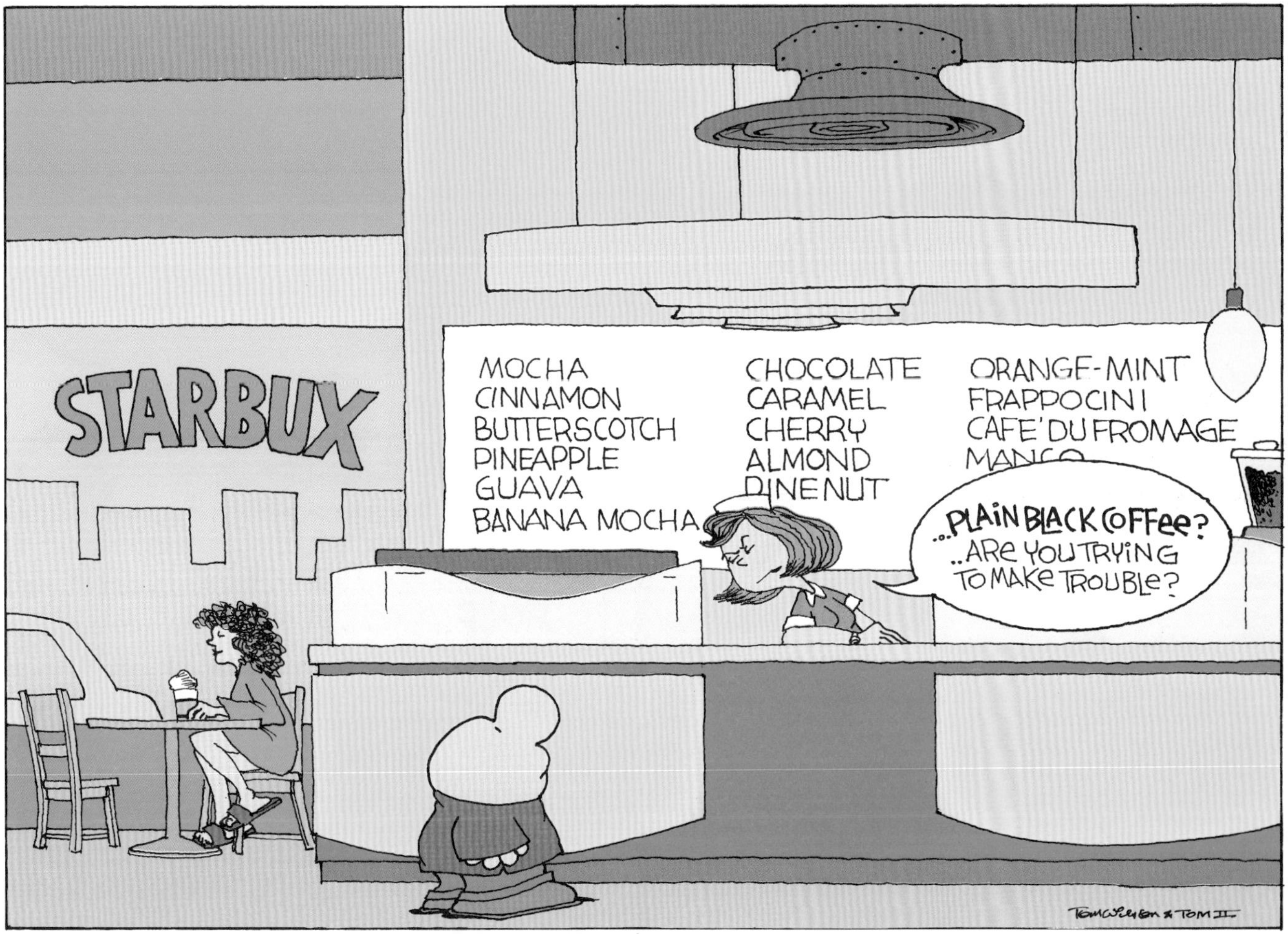
STARBUX
MOCHA
CINNAMON
BUTTERSCOTCH
PINEAPPLE
GUAVA
BANANA MOCHA
CHOCOLATE
CARAMEL
CHERRY
ALMOND
PINENUT
ORANGE-MINT
FRAPPOCINI
CAFE' DU FROMAGE
...PLAIN BLACK COFFEE? ...ARE YOU TRYING TO MAKE TROUBLE?

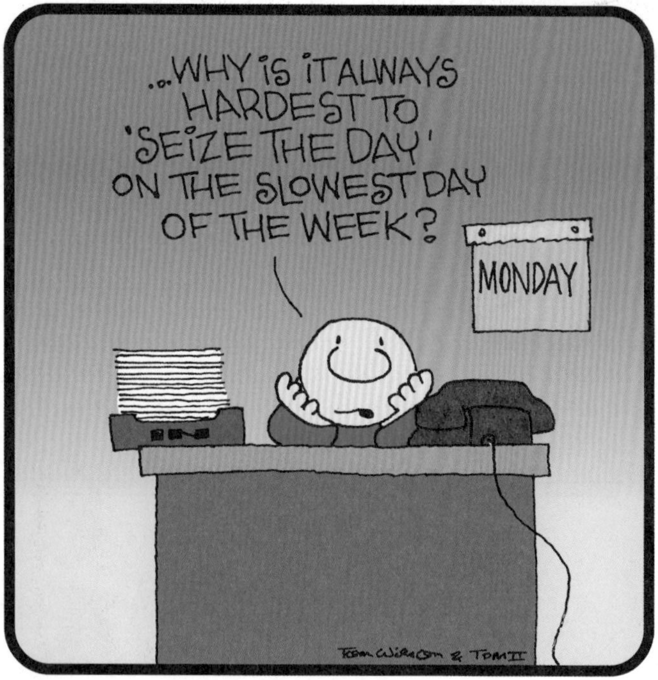
...WHY IS IT ALWAYS HARDEST TO 'SEIZE THE DAY' ON THE SLOWEST DAY OF THE WEEK?
MONDAY

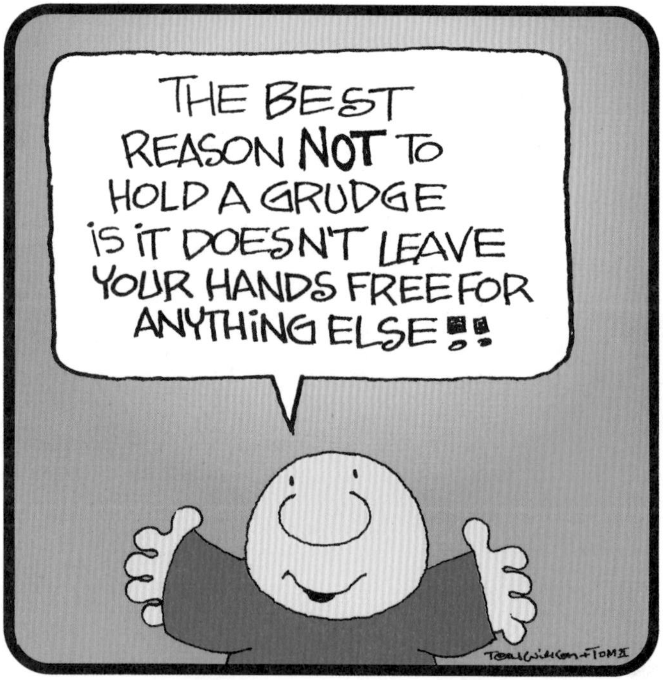
THE BEST REASON NOT TO HOLD A GRUDGE IS IT DOESN'T LEAVE YOUR HANDS FREE FOR ANYTHING ELSE!!

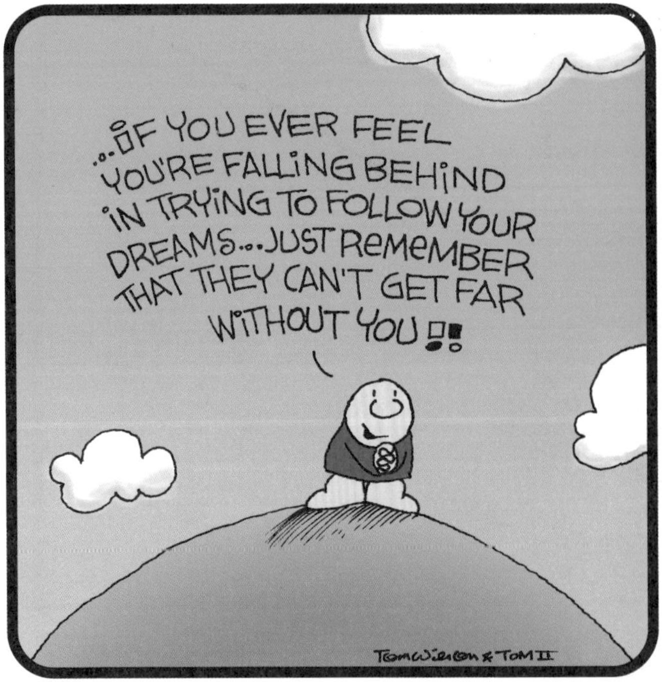
...IF YOU EVER FEEL YOU'RE FALLING BEHIND IN TRYING TO FOLLOW YOUR DREAMS...JUST REMEMBER THAT THEY CAN'T GET FAR WITHOUT YOU!!
Tom Wilson & TOM II

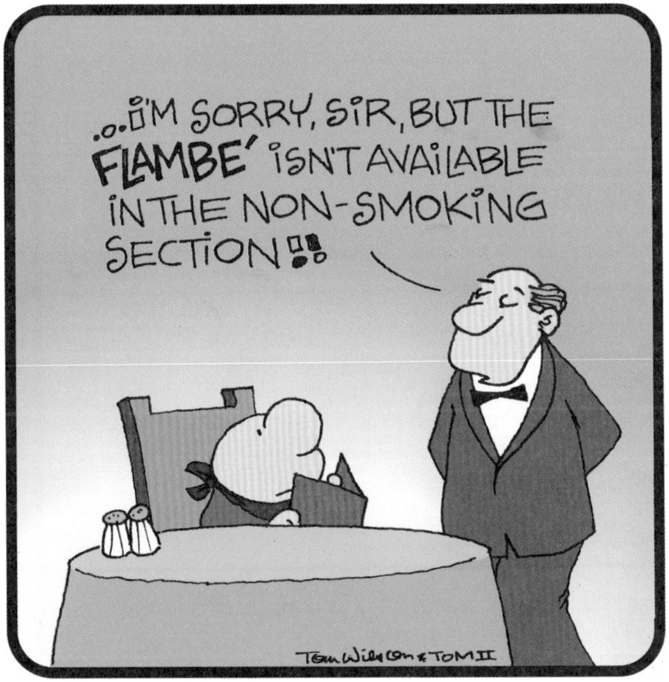
...I'M SORRY, SIR, BUT THE FLAMBE' ISN'T AVAILABLE IN THE NON-SMOKING SECTION!!
Tom Wilson & TOM II

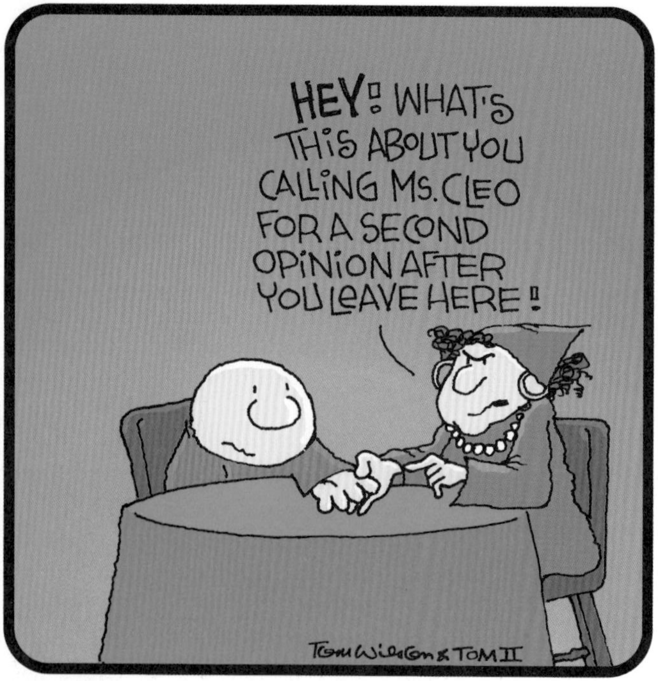
HEY! WHAT'S THIS ABOUT YOU CALLING MS. CLEO FOR A SECOND OPINION AFTER YOU LEAVE HERE!
Tom Wilson & Tom II

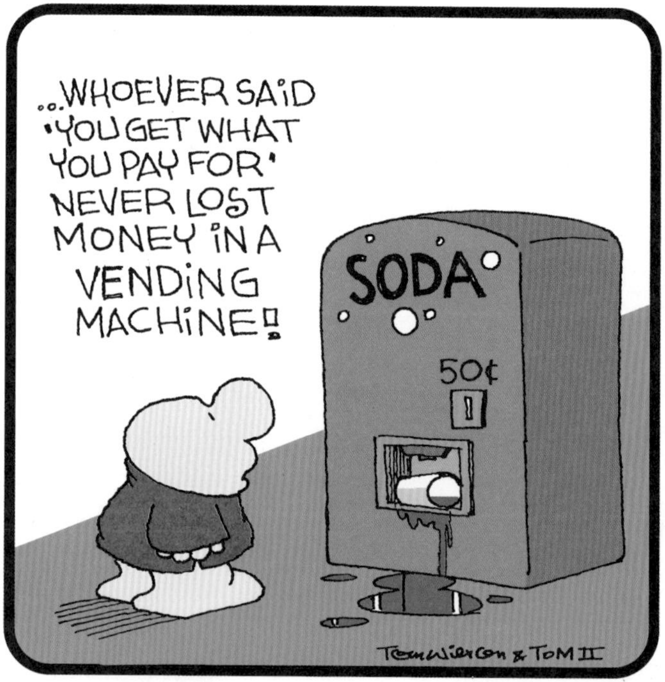
...WHOEVER SAID 'YOU GET WHAT YOU PAY FOR' NEVER LOST MONEY IN A VENDING MACHINE!
SODA
50¢
Tom Wilson & Tom II

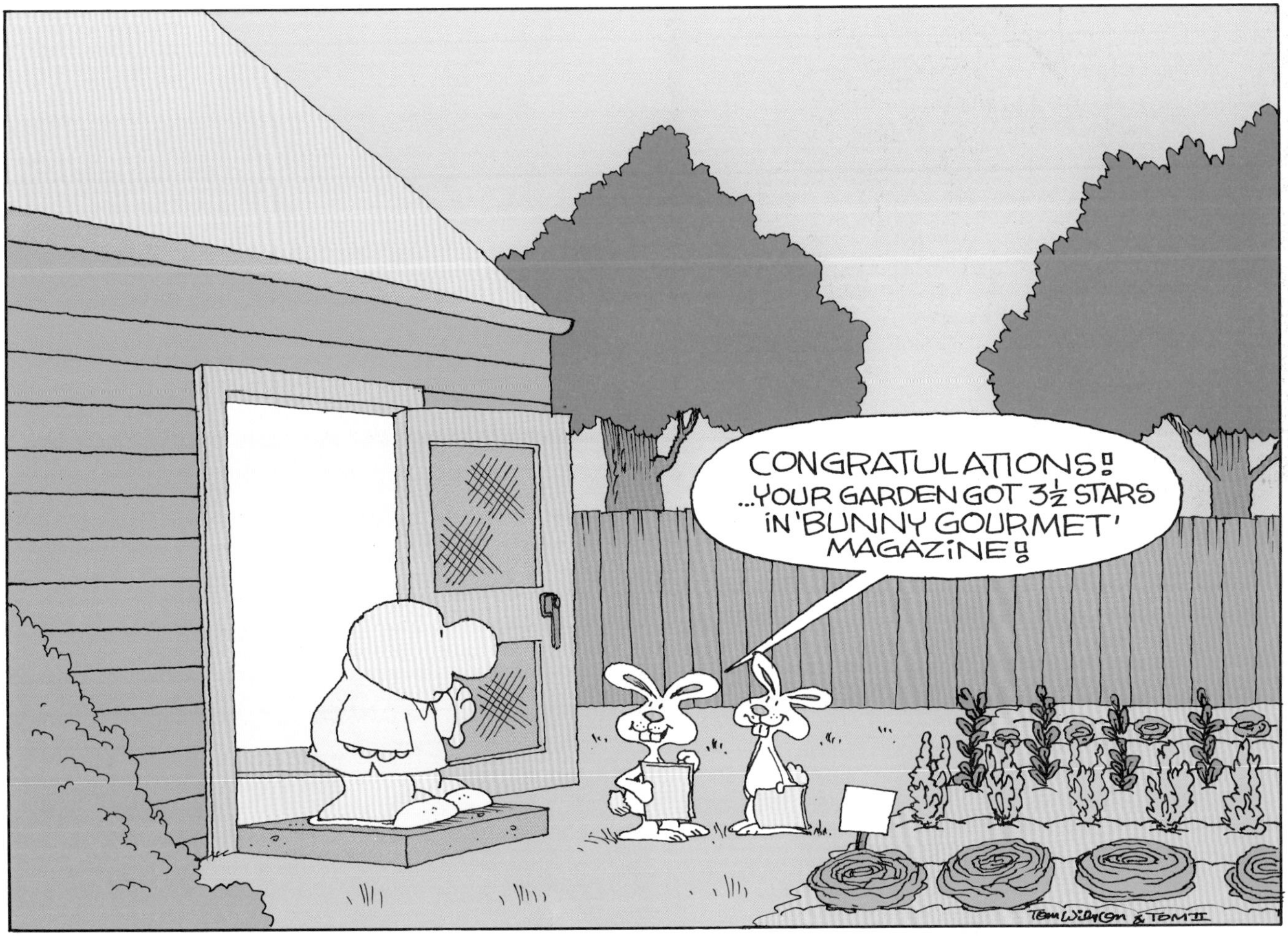
CONGRATULATIONS!
...YOUR GARDEN GOT 3½ STARS
IN 'BUNNY GOURMET'
MAGAZINE!
TOM WILSON & TOM II

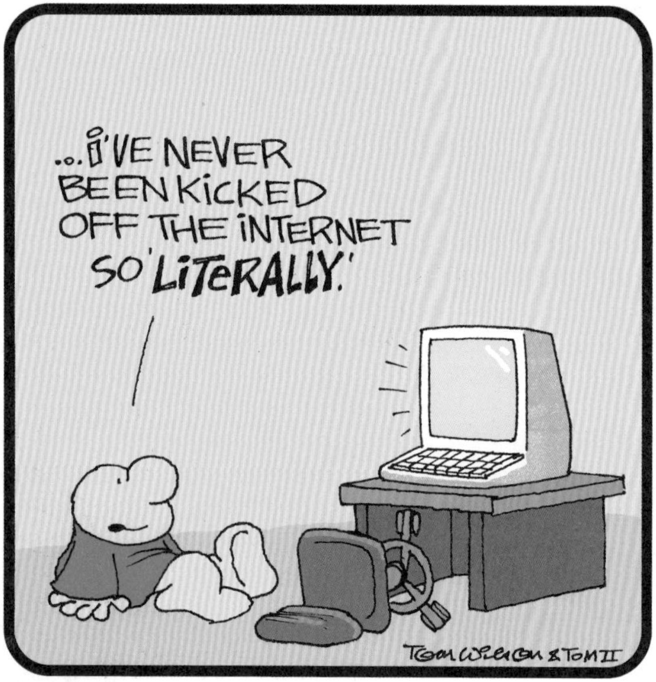
..I'VE NEVER BEEN KICKED OFF THE INTERNET SO 'LITERALLY.'
TOM WILSON & TOM II

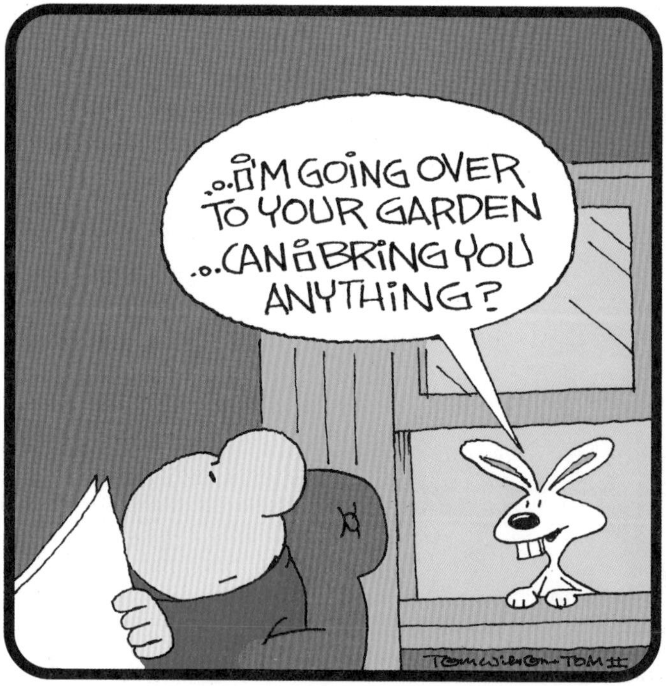
..I'M GOING OVER TO YOUR GARDEN ..CAN I BRING YOU ANYTHING?
TOM WILSON-TOM II

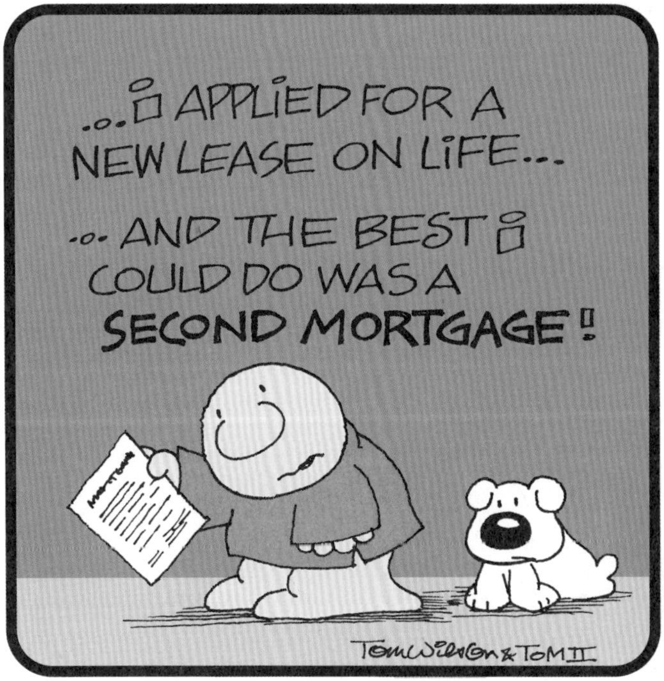
...I APPLIED FOR A NEW LEASE ON LIFE...
...AND THE BEST I COULD DO WAS A SECOND MORTGAGE!
Tom Wilson & Tom II

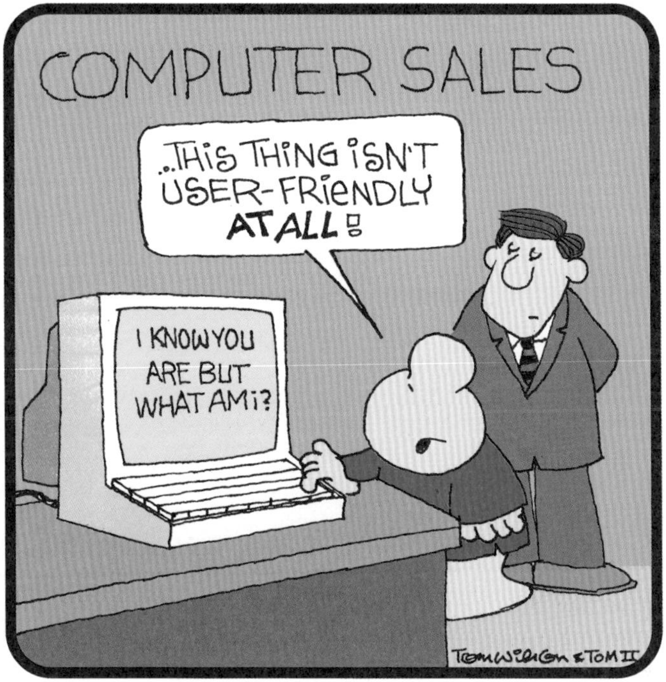
COMPUTER SALES
..THIS THING ISN'T USER-FRIENDLY AT ALL!
I KNOW YOU ARE BUT WHAT AM I?
Tom Wilson & Tom II

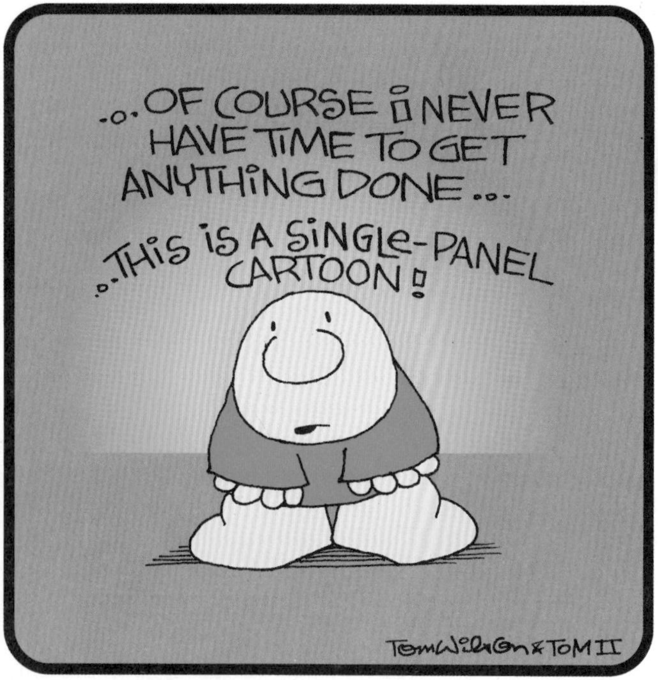
..OF COURSE I NEVER HAVE TIME TO GET ANYTHING DONE...
..THIS IS A SINGLE-PANEL CARTOON!
TOM WILSON & TOM II

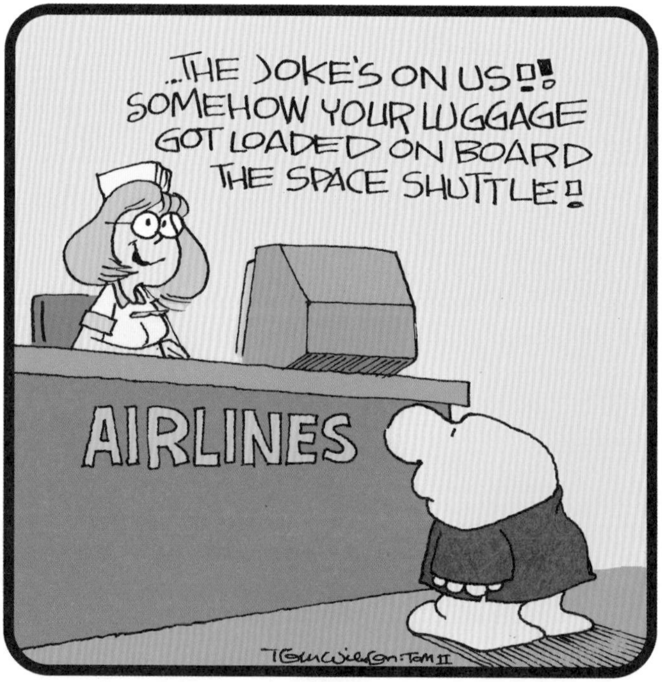
..THE JOKE'S ON US!! SOMEHOW YOUR LUGGAGE GOT LOADED ON BOARD THE SPACE SHUTTLE!
AIRLINES
TOM WILSON: TOM II

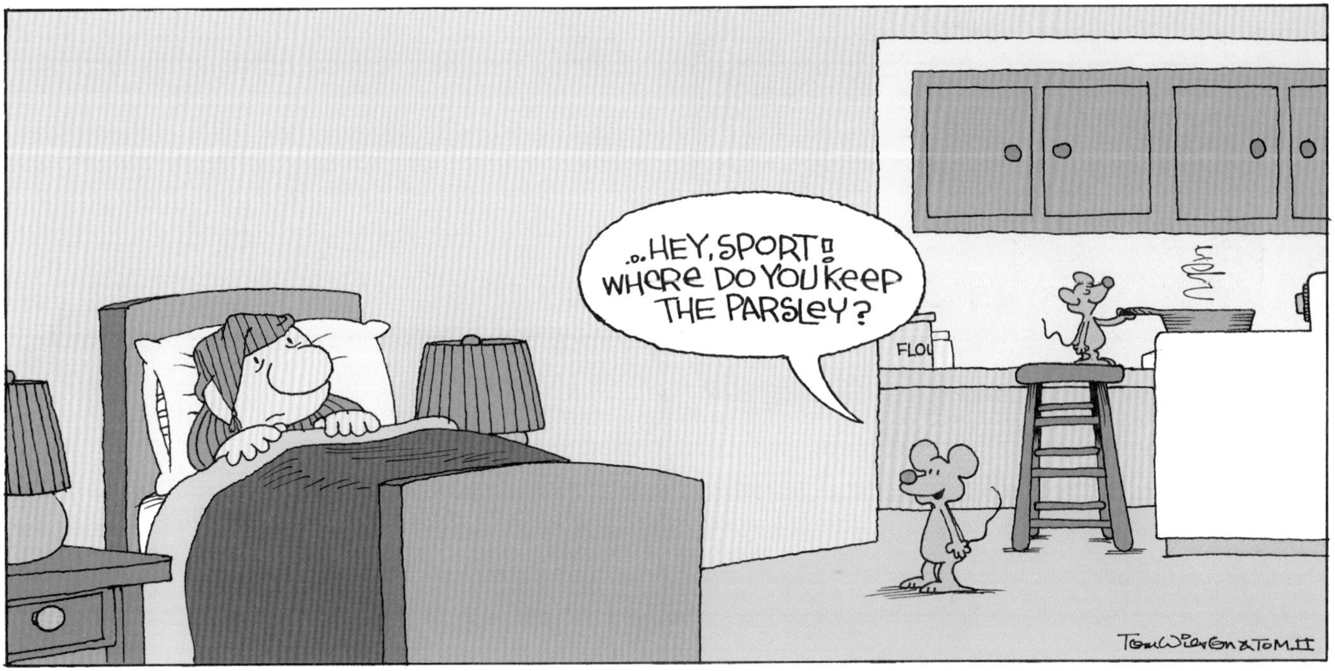
...HEY, SPORT!! WHERE DO YOU KEEP THE PARSLEY?
FLOU
TOM WILSON & TOM II

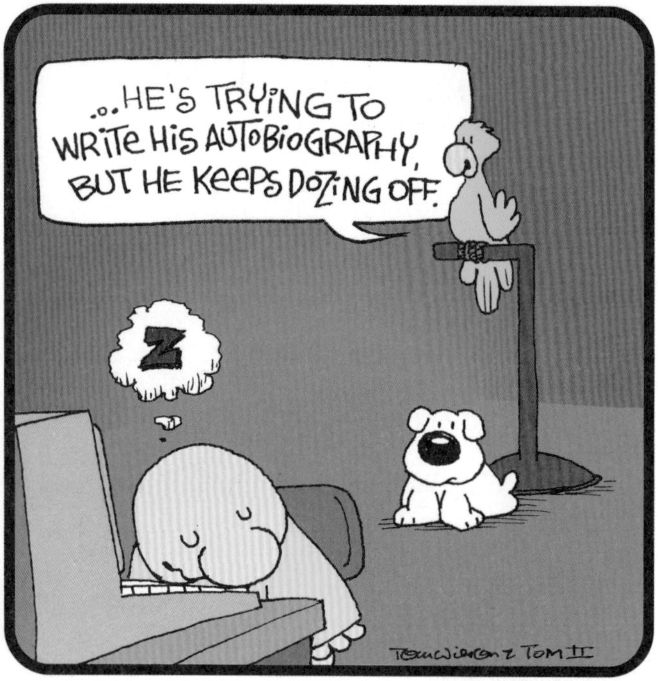
..HE'S TRYING TO WRITE HIS AUTOBIOGRAPHY, BUT HE KEEPS DOZING OFF.
Z
TOM WILSON & TOM II

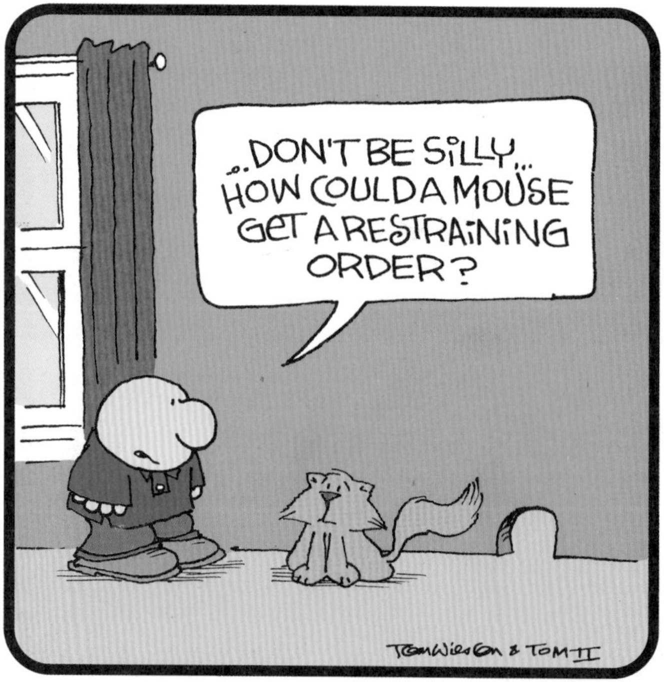
..DON'T BE SILLY... HOW COULD A MOUSE GET A RESTRAINING ORDER?
TOM WILSON & TOM II

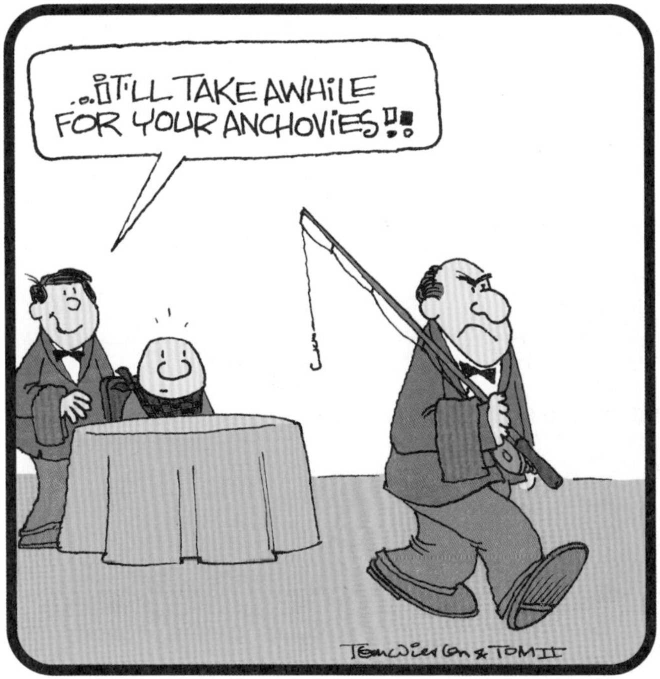
..IT'LL TAKE AWHILE FOR YOUR ANCHOVIES!!
TOM WILSON & TOM II

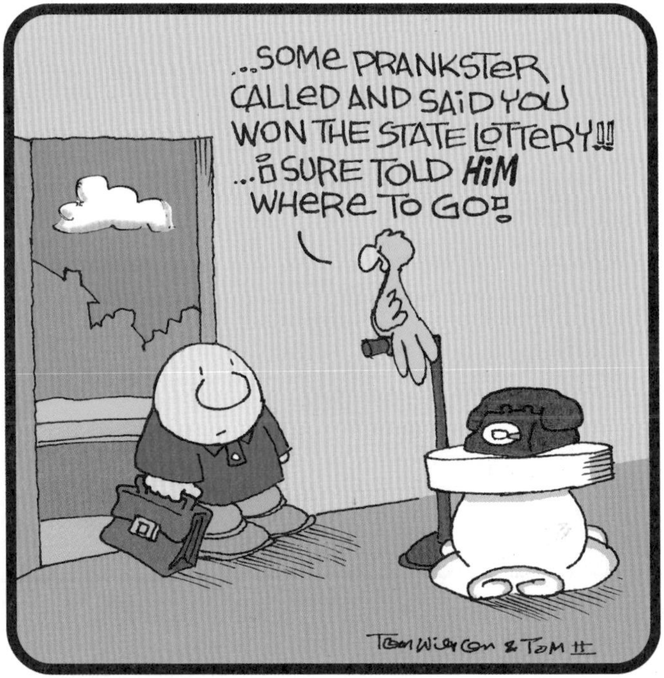
...SOME PRANKSTER CALLED AND SAID YOU WON THE STATE LOTTERY!! ...I SURE TOLD HIM WHERE TO GO!
TOM WILSON & TOM II

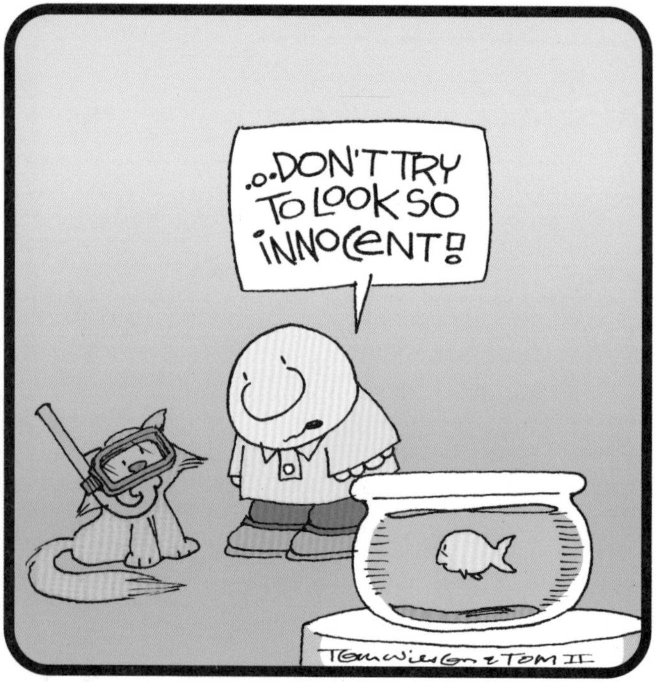
..o..DON'T TRY TO LOOK SO INNOCENT!!
TOM WILSON & TOM II

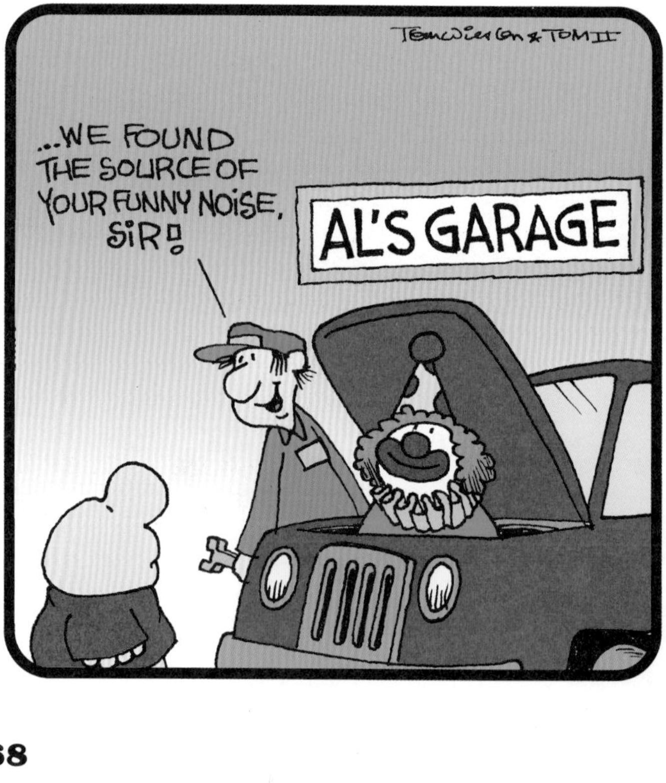
TOM WILSON & TOM II
...WE FOUND THE SOURCE OF YOUR FUNNY NOISE, SIR!!
AL'S GARAGE

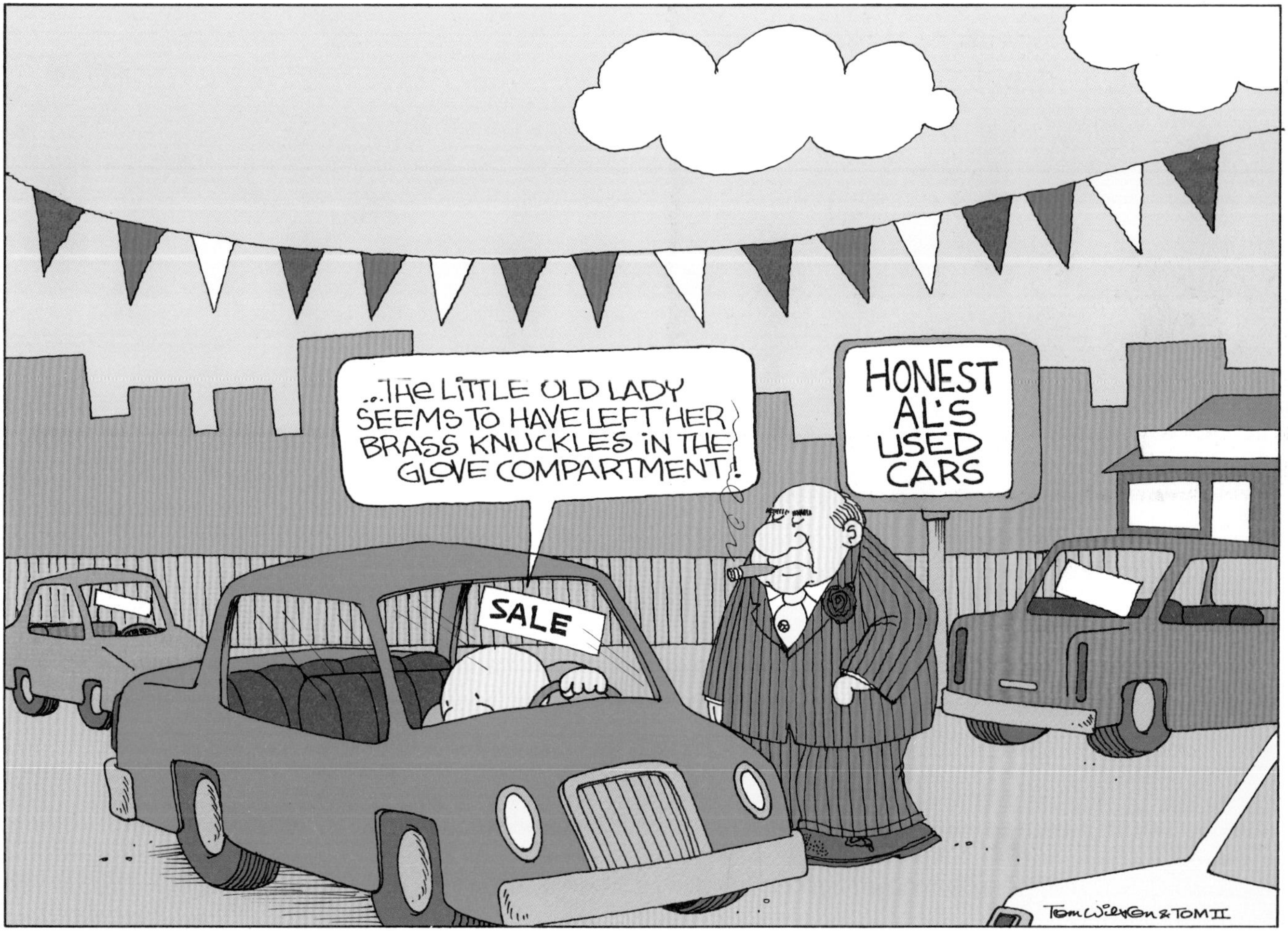
...THE LITTLE OLD LADY SEEMS TO HAVE LEFT HER BRASS KNUCKLES IN THE GLOVE COMPARTMENT!
HONEST AL'S USED CARS
SALE
Tom Wilson & TOM II

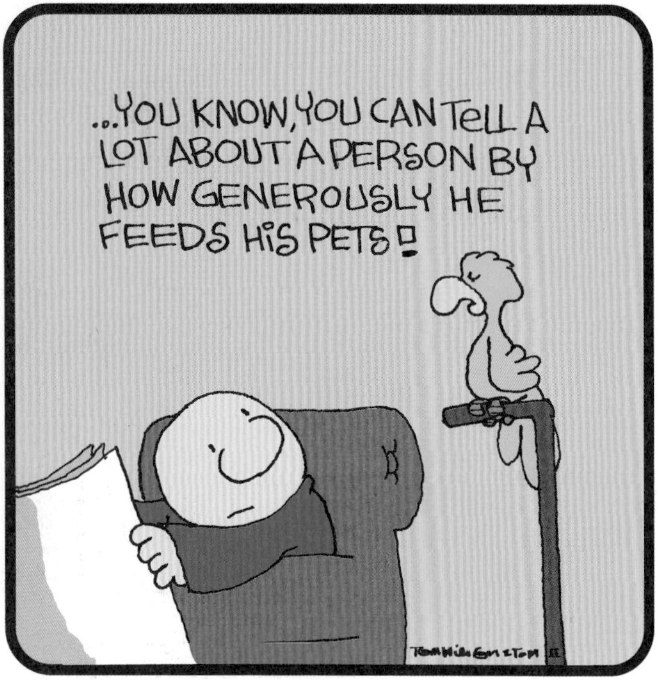
..YOU KNOW, YOU CAN TELL A LOT ABOUT A PERSON BY HOW GENEROUSLY HE FEEDS HIS PETS!!

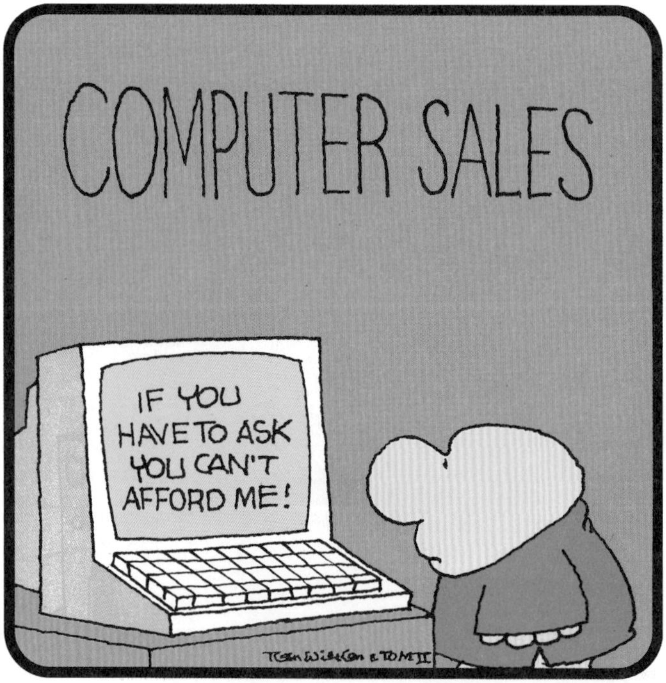
COMPUTER SALES
IF YOU HAVE TO ASK YOU CAN'T AFFORD ME!

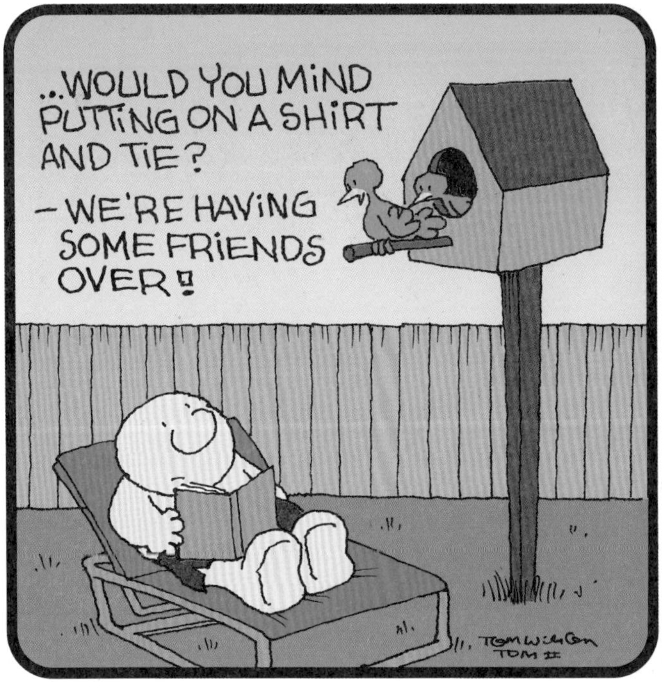
...WOULD YOU MIND PUTTING ON A SHIRT AND TIE?
-WE'RE HAVING SOME FRIENDS OVER!

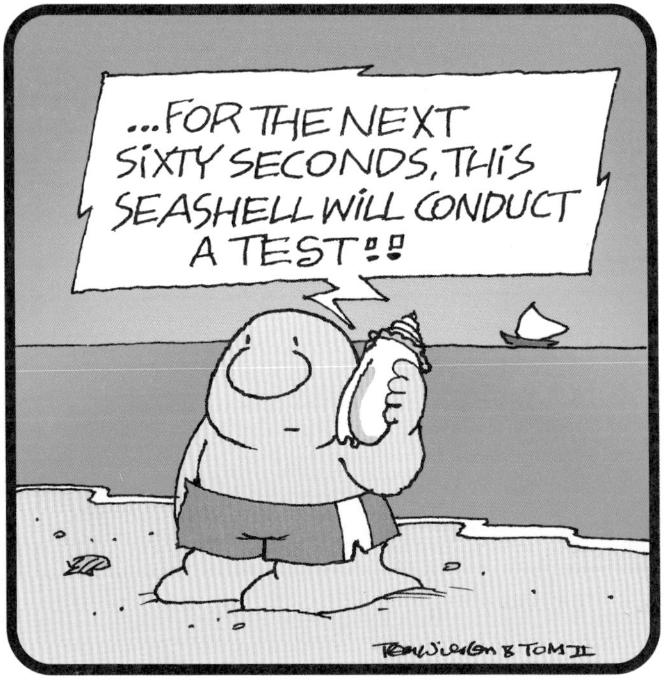
...FOR THE NEXT SIXTY SECONDS, THIS SEASHELL WILL CONDUCT A TEST!!

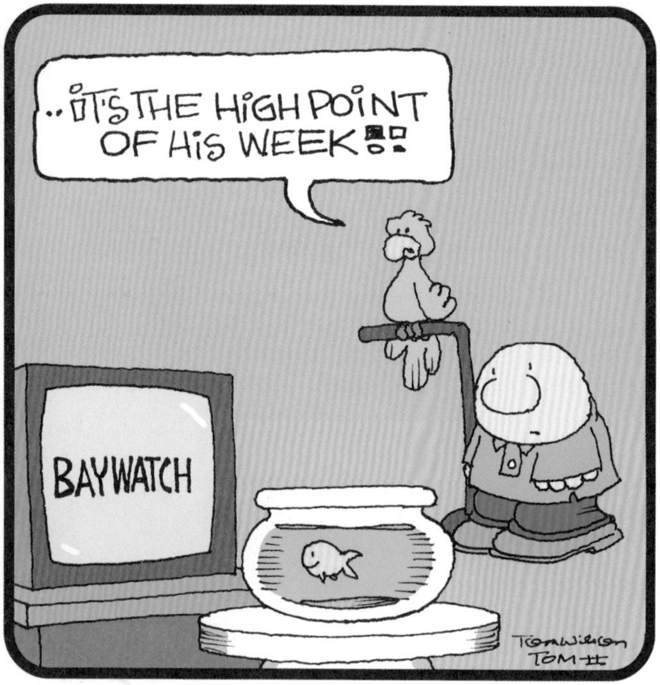
..IT'S THE HIGH POINT OF HIS WEEK!!
BAYWATCH
Tom Wilson TOM II

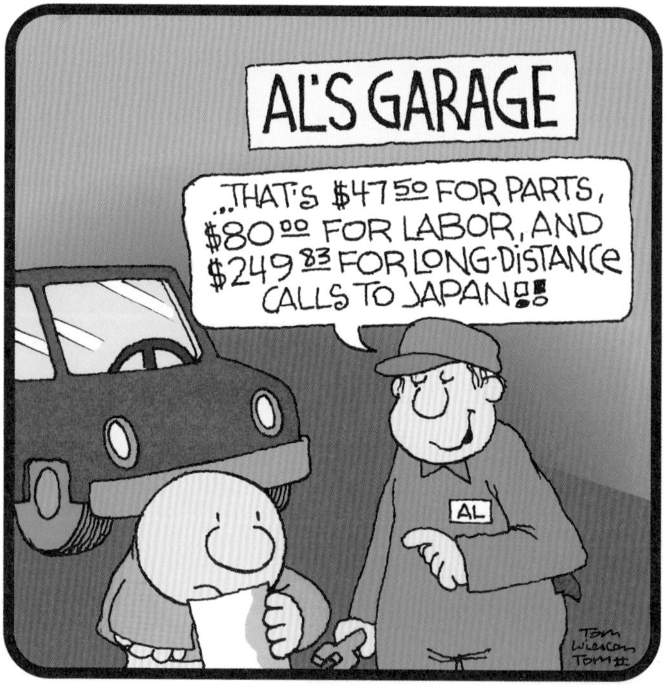
AL'S GARAGE
...THAT'S $47 50 FOR PARTS, $80 00 FOR LABOR, AND $249 83 FOR LONG-DISTANCE CALLS TO JAPAN!!
AL
Tom Wilson TOM II

...I'LL NEVER UNDERSTAND WHY "GO FLY A KITE" IS CONSIDERED SUCH AN INSULT !!

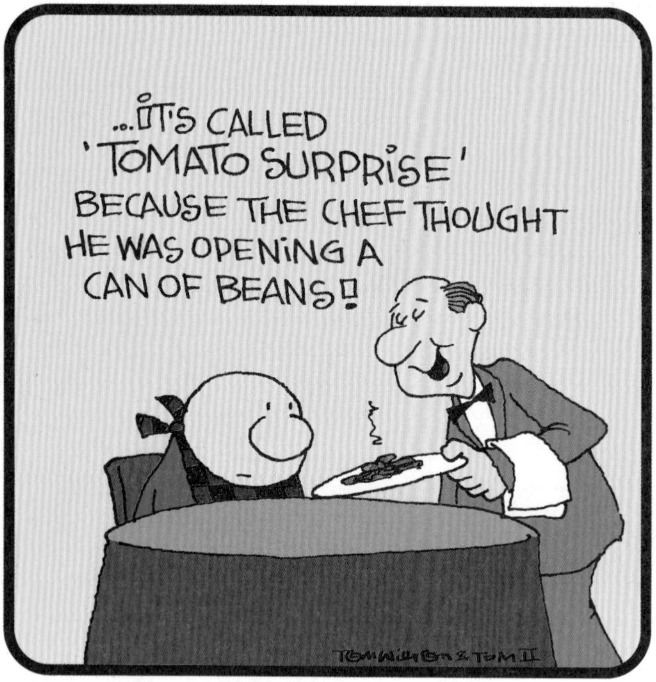
...IT'S CALLED 'TOMATO SURPRISE' BECAUSE THE CHEF THOUGHT HE WAS OPENING A CAN OF BEANS!
TOM WILSON & TOM II

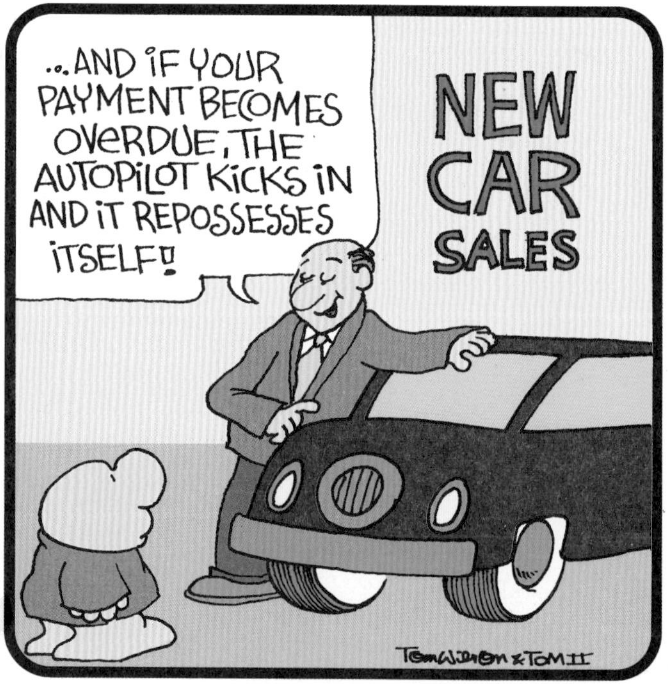
...AND IF YOUR PAYMENT BECOMES OVERDUE, THE AUTOPILOT KICKS IN AND IT REPOSSESSES ITSELF!
NEW CAR SALES
TOM WILSON & TOM II

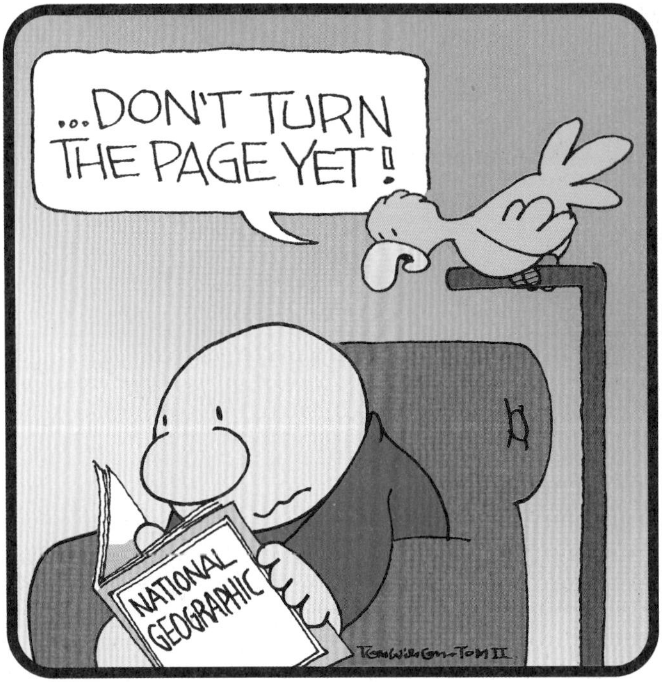
...DON'T TURN THE PAGE YET!
NATIONAL GEOGRAPHIC

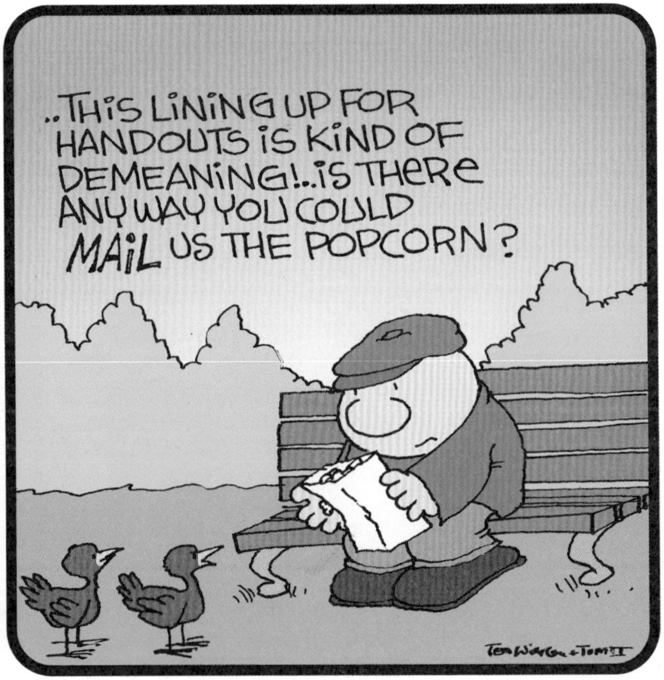
..THIS LINING UP FOR HANDOUTS IS KIND OF DEMEANING!..IS THERE ANY WAY YOU COULD MAIL US THE POPCORN?

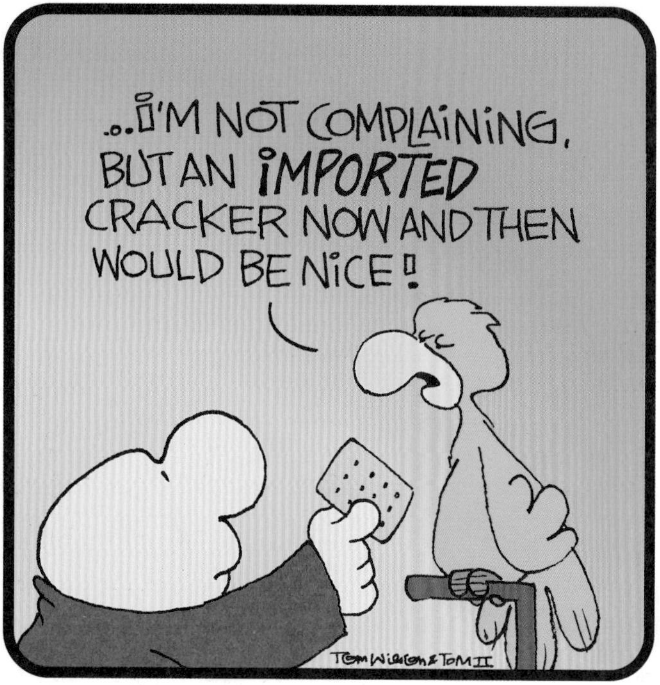
..I'M NOT COMPLAINING, BUT AN IMPORTED CRACKER NOW AND THEN WOULD BE NICE!
TOM WILSON & TOM II

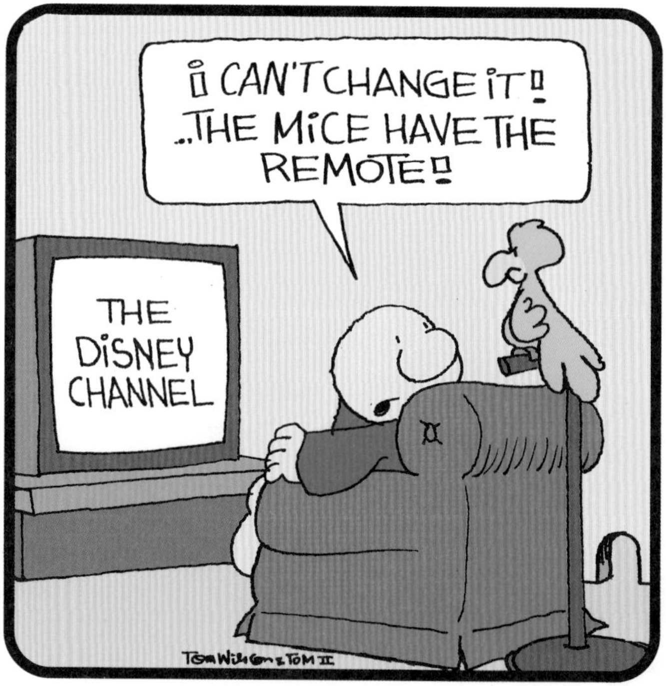
I CAN'T CHANGE IT! ..THE MICE HAVE THE REMOTE!
THE DISNEY CHANNEL
TOM WILSON & TOM II

MORNIN' SIGGIE..
..ER, DO YOU HAVE AN ACCOUNT WITH US, SIR ?
TELLER
YES, FIFTEEN YEARS!
..ER.. HOW LONG HAVE YOU BEEN WITH US MR...UH..
ZIGGY, SIR.
MGR.
PSYCHIATRIST
DOCTOR..ER MR. WHATSHISNAME IS HERE FOR HIS APPOINTMENT!
..SOME PEOPLE NEED NO INTRODUCTION..
..I'M ONE OF THOSE WHO NEED MORE THAN ONE!!
TOM WILSON & TOM II

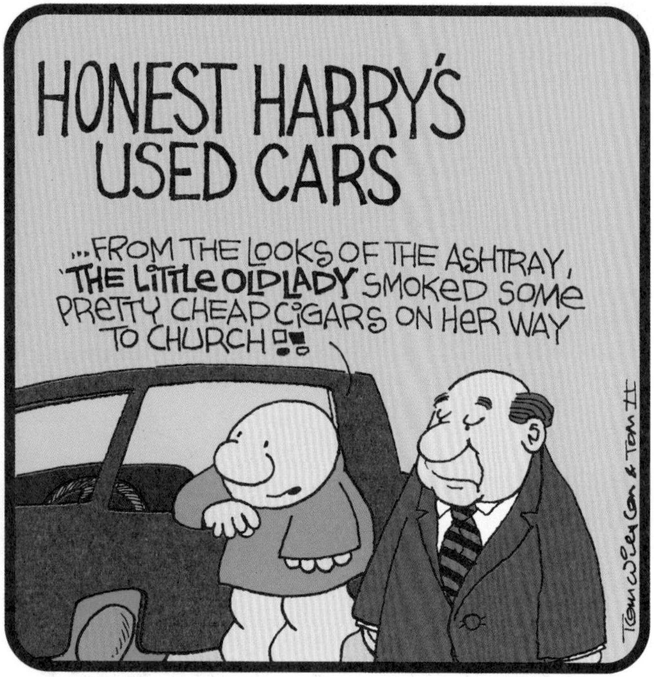
HONEST HARRY'S
USED CARS
...FROM THE LOOKS OF THE ASHTRAY, 'THE LITTLE OLD LADY' SMOKED SOME PRETTY CHEAP CIGARS ON HER WAY TO CHURCH!?!
Tom Wilson & Tom II

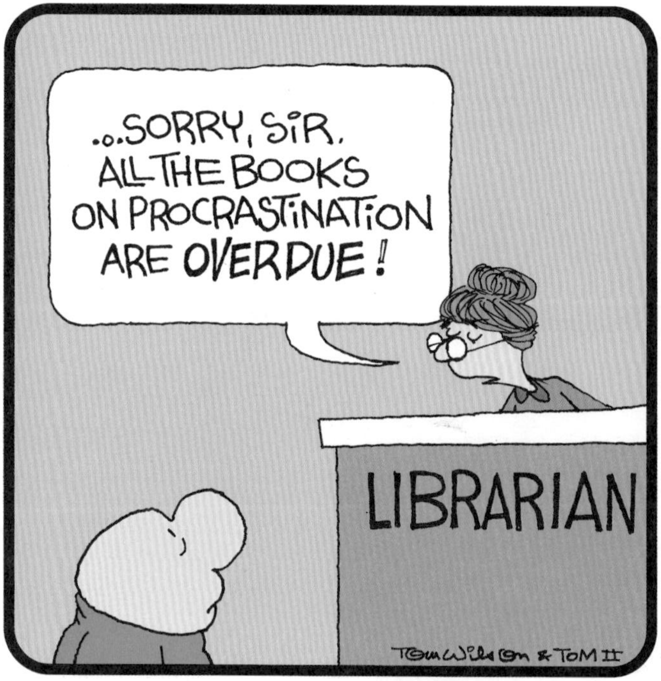
...SORRY, SIR. ALL THE BOOKS ON PROCRASTINATION ARE OVERDUE!
LIBRARIAN
Tom Wilson & Tom II

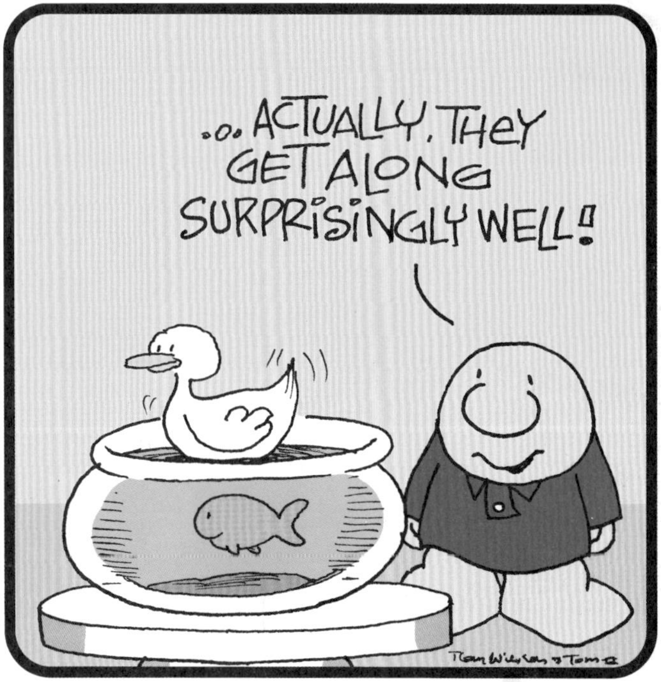
..o.. ACTUALLY, THEY GET ALONG SURPRISINGLY WELL!
Tom Wilson & Tom II

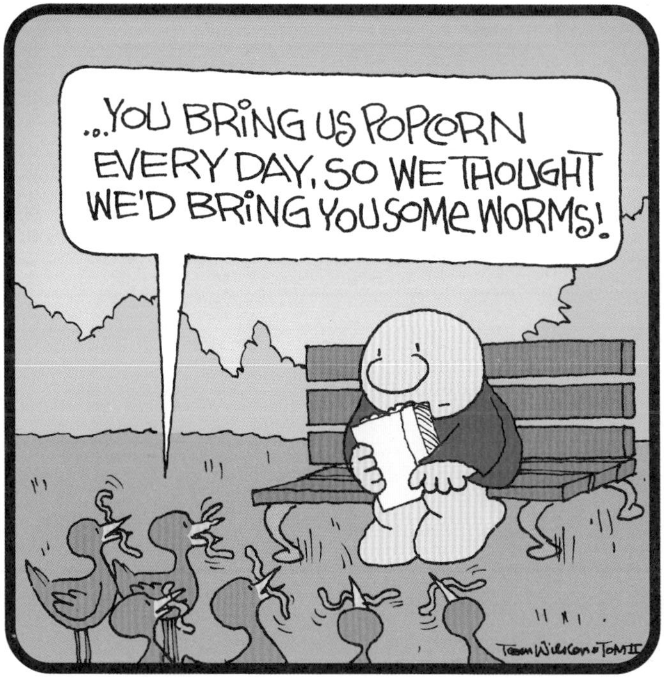
...YOU BRING US POPCORN EVERY DAY, SO WE THOUGHT WE'D BRING YOU SOME WORMS!
Tom Wilson & Tom II

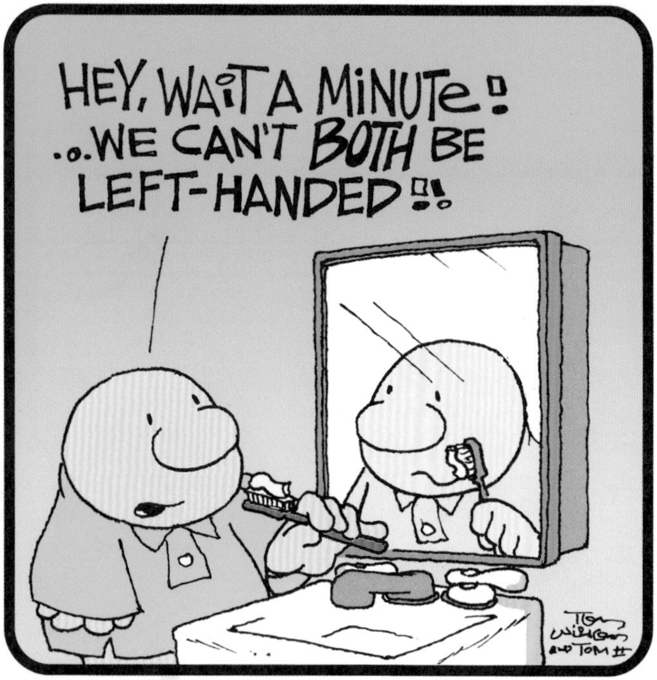
HEY, WAIT A MINUTE!
..WE CAN'T BOTH BE LEFT-HANDED!!
TOM WILSON AND TOM II

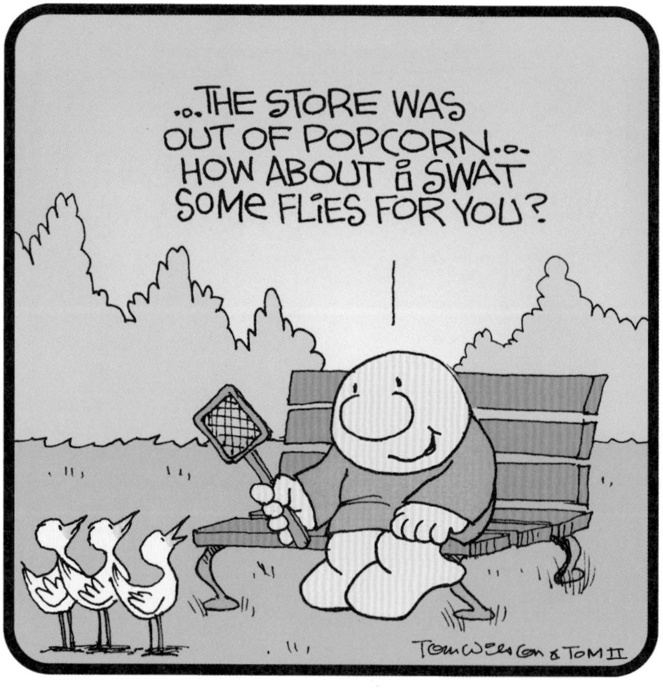
..THE STORE WAS OUT OF POPCORN.. HOW ABOUT I SWAT SOME FLIES FOR YOU?
TOM WILSON & TOM II

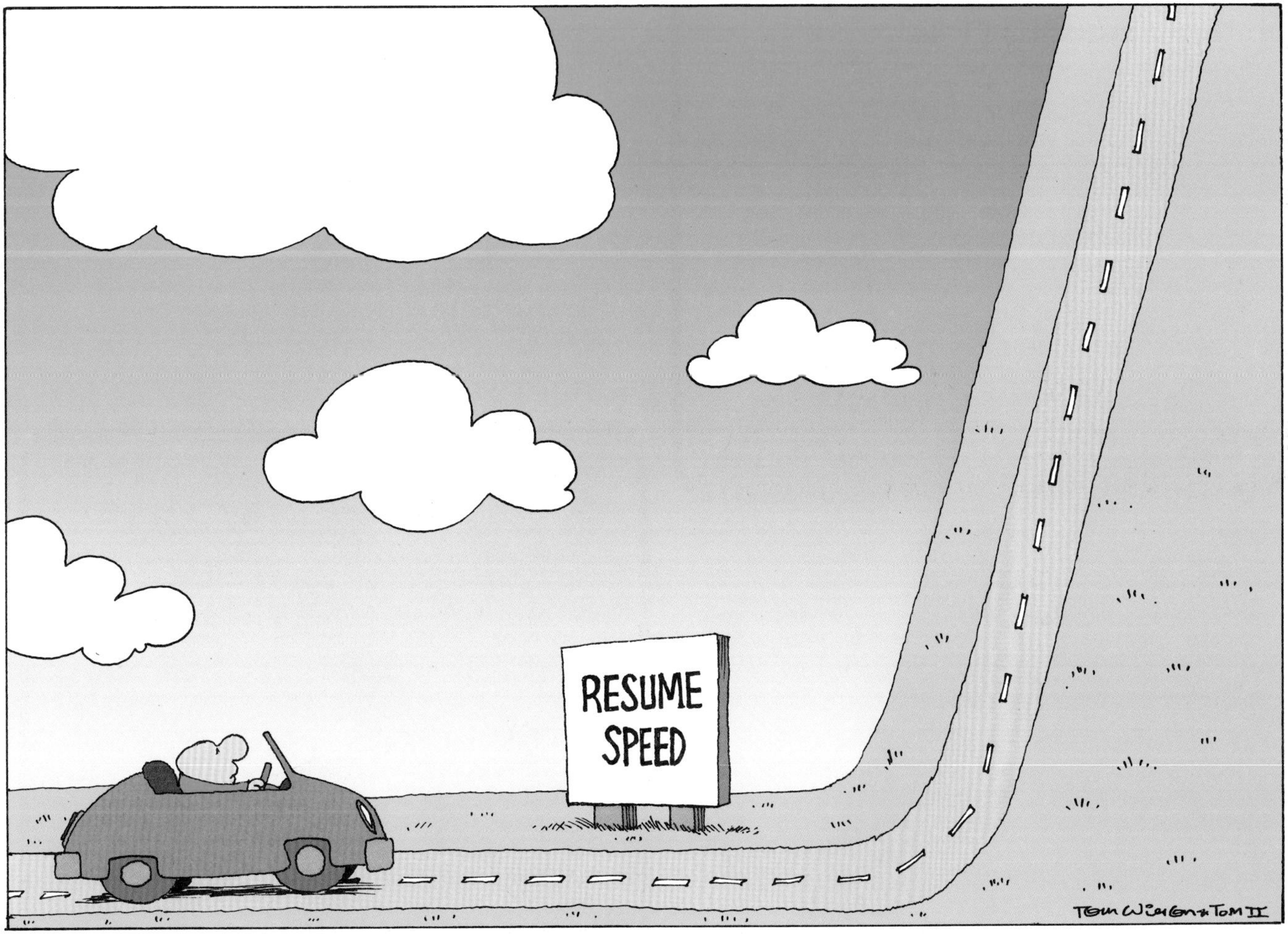
RESUME
SPEED
TOM WILSON & TOM II

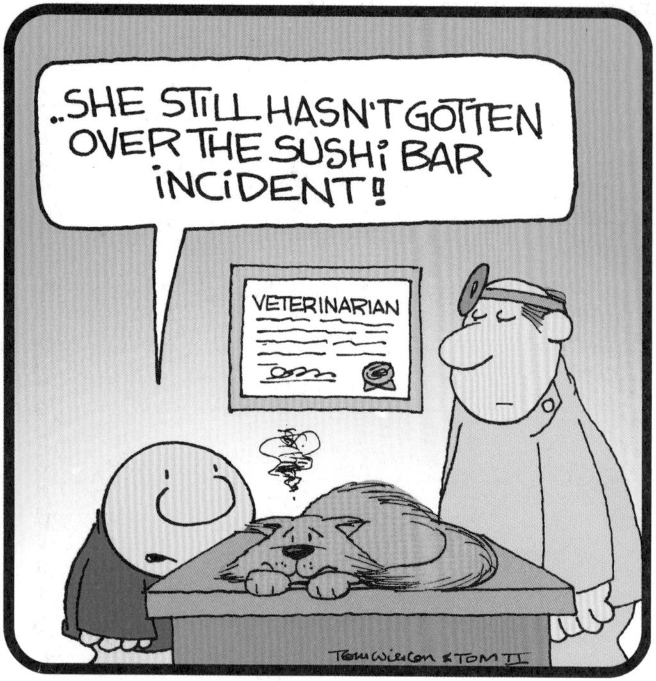
..SHE STILL HASN'T GOTTEN OVER THE SUSHI BAR INCIDENT!
VETERINARIAN
TOM WILSON & TOM II

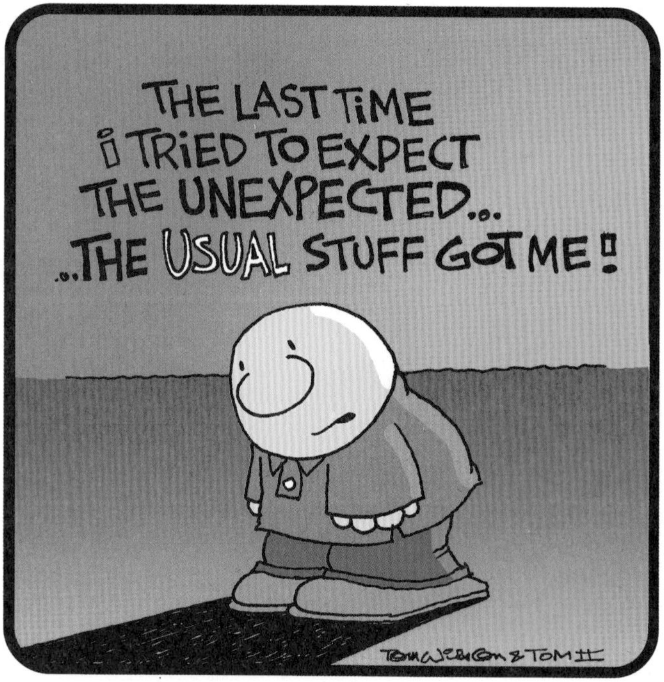
THE LAST TIME I TRIED TO EXPECT THE UNEXPECTED...
..THE USUAL STUFF GOT ME!
TOM WILSON & TOM II

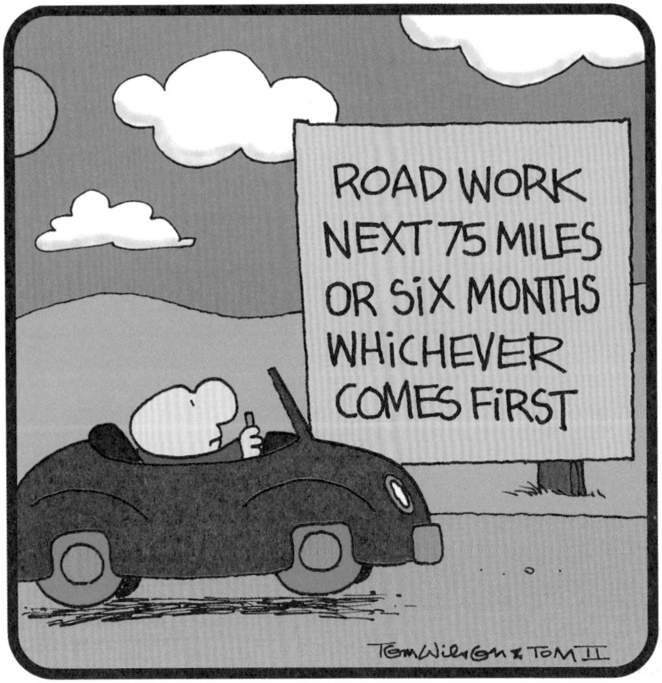
ROAD WORK
NEXT 75 MILES
OR SIX MONTHS
WHICHEVER
COMES FIRST
TOM WILSON & TOM II

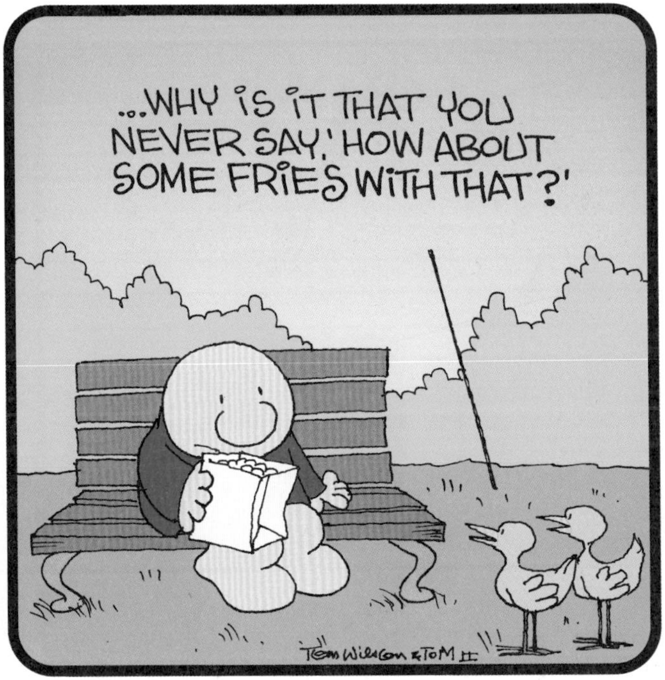
...WHY IS IT THAT YOU NEVER SAY, 'HOW ABOUT SOME FRIES WITH THAT?'
TOM WILSON & TOM II

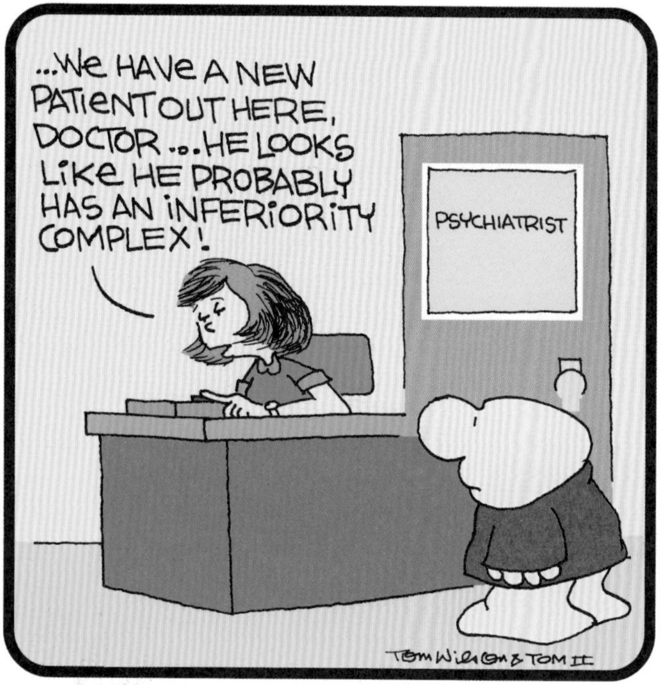
...WE HAVE A NEW PATIENT OUT HERE, DOCTOR ... HE LOOKS LIKE HE PROBABLY HAS AN INFERIORITY COMPLEX!
PSYCHIATRIST
TOM WILSON & TOM II

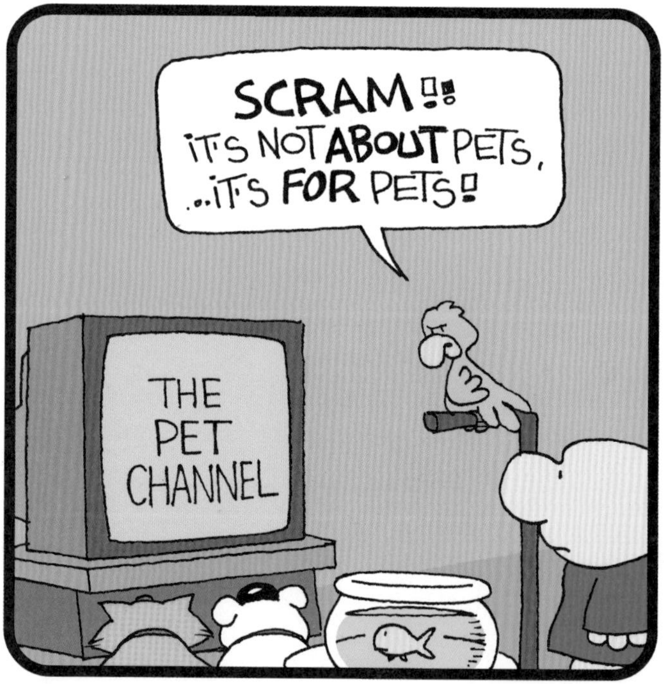
SCRAM!!! IT'S NOT ABOUT PETS, ...IT'S FOR PETS!
THE PET CHANNEL

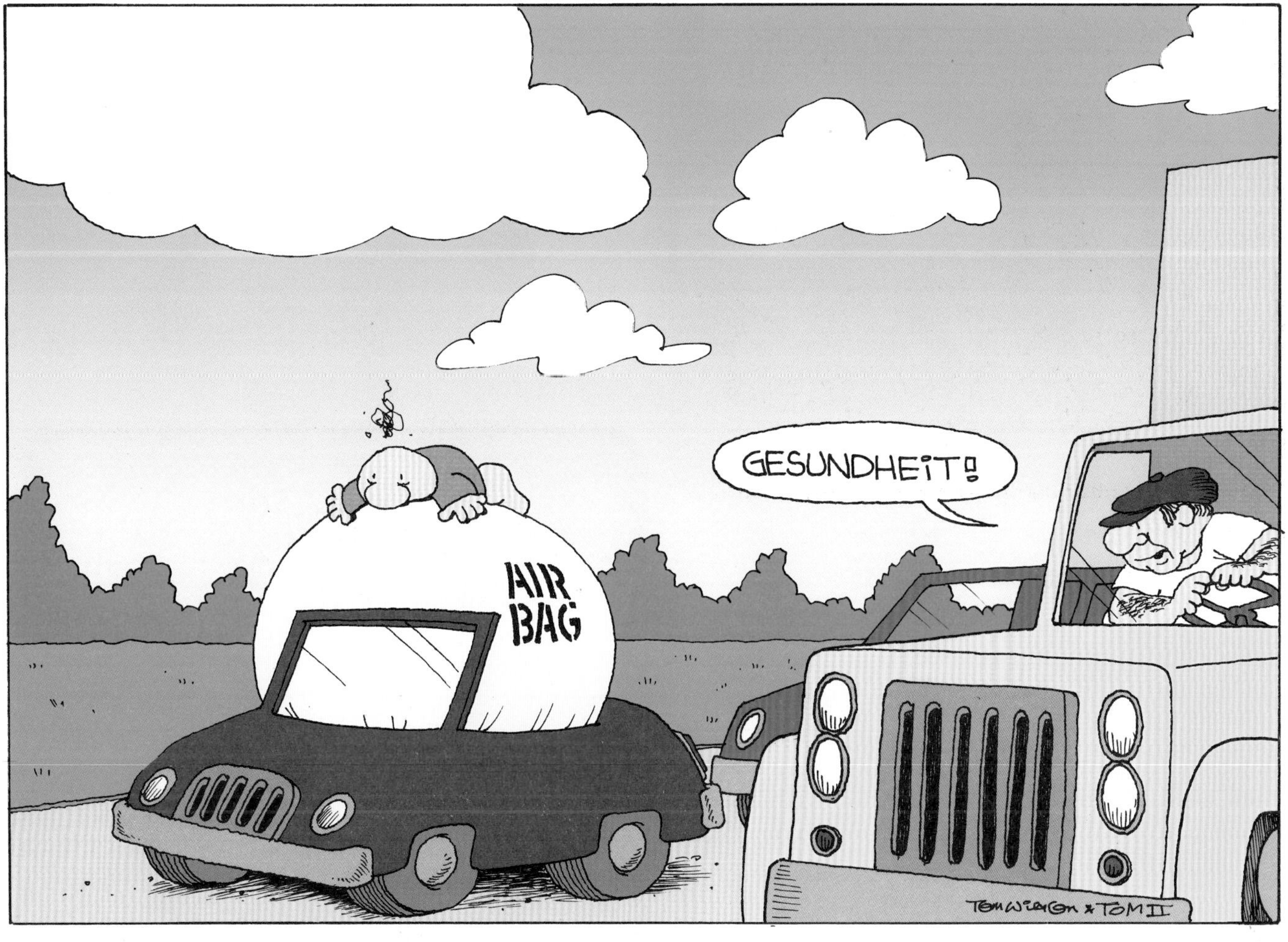
AIR
BAG
GESUNDHEIT!
TOM WILSON & TOM II

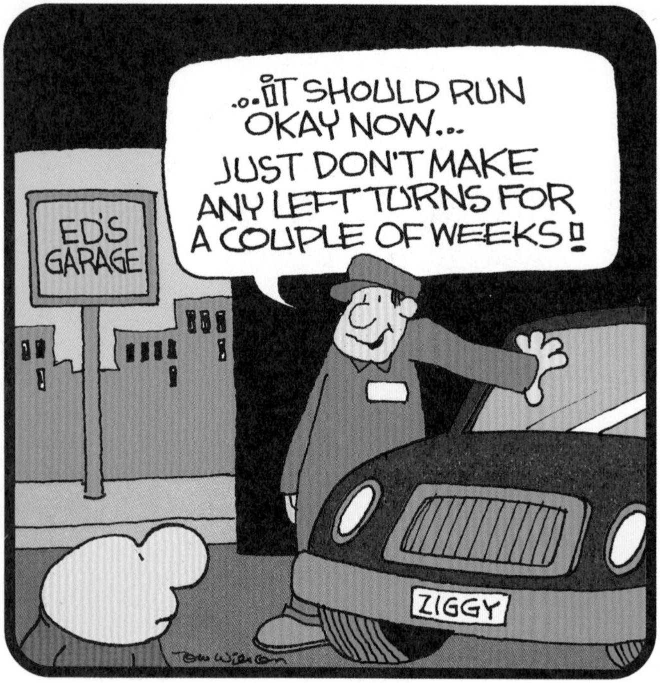
..o..IT SHOULD RUN OKAY NOW... JUST DON'T MAKE ANY LEFT TURNS FOR A COUPLE OF WEEKS!
ED'S GARAGE
ZIGGY
Tom Wilson

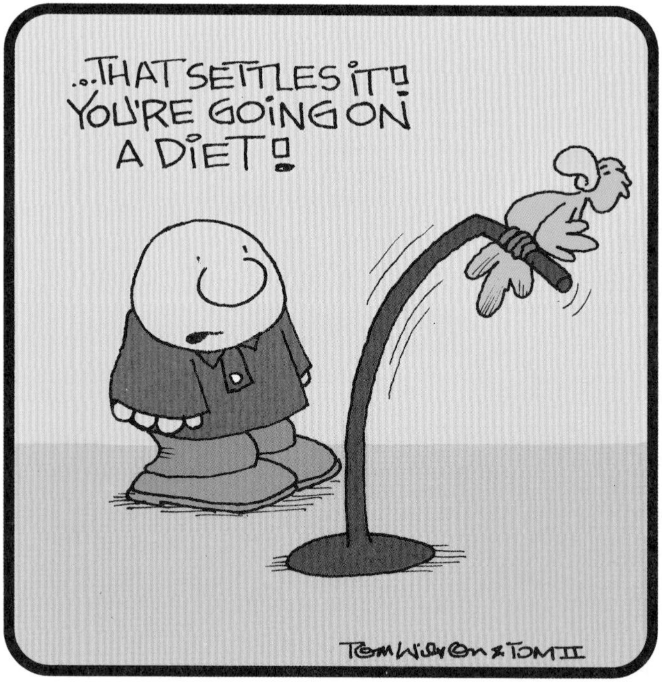
..THAT SETTLES IT! YOU'RE GOING ON A DIET!
Tom Wilson & Tom II

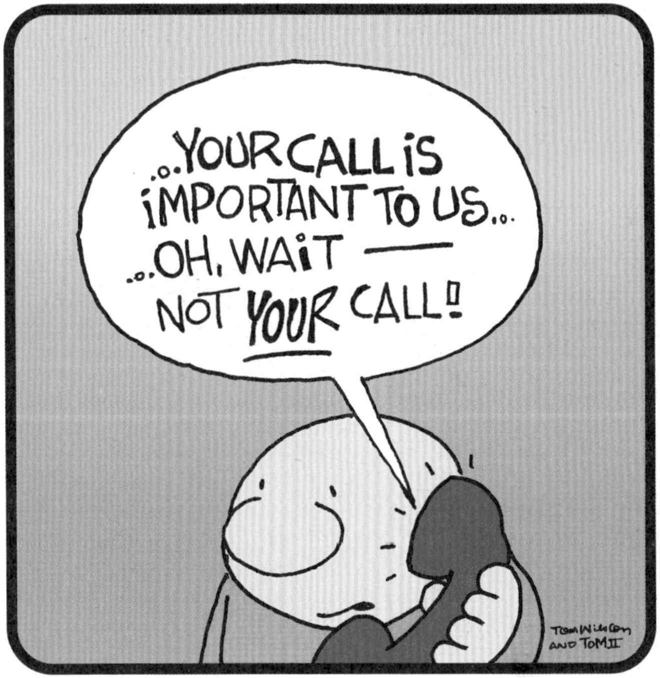
..o.YOUR CALL IS IMPORTANT TO US..o. ..o.OH, WAIT — NOT YOUR CALL!
TOM WILSON AND TOM II

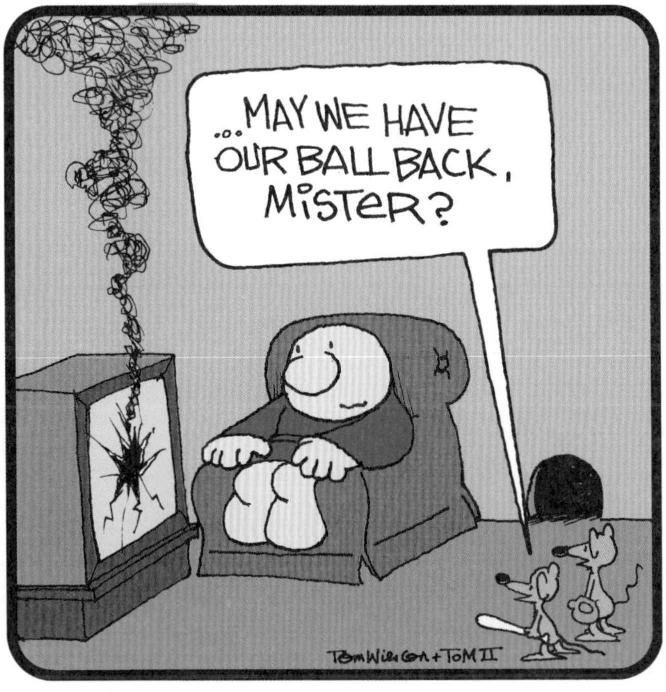
..o.MAY WE HAVE OUR BALL BACK, MISTER?
TOM WILSON + TOM II

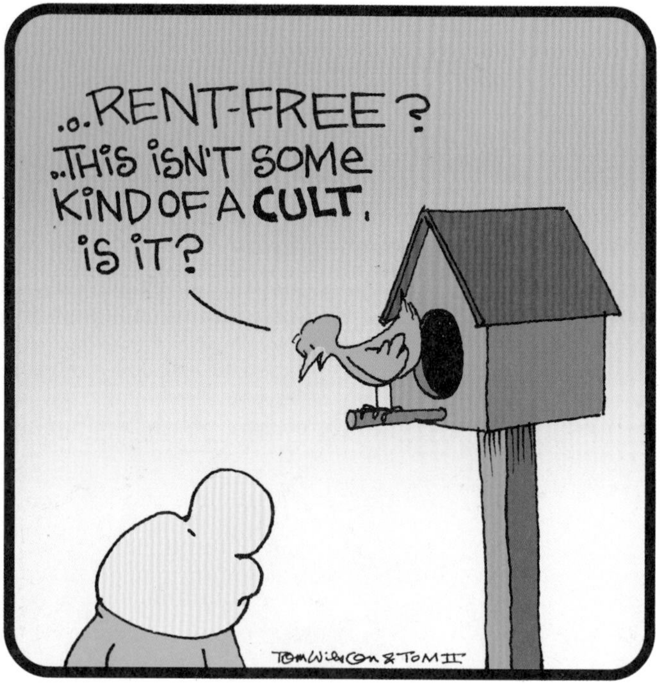
..o..RENT-FREE?
..THIS ISN'T SOME KIND OF A **CULT**, IS IT?
TOM WILSON & TOM II

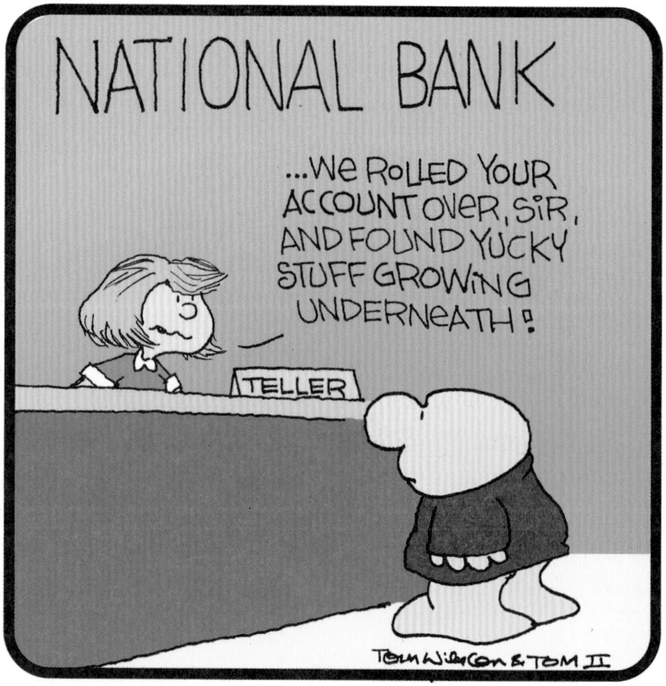
NATIONAL BANK
...WE ROLLED YOUR ACCOUNT OVER, SIR, AND FOUND YUCKY STUFF GROWING UNDERNEATH!
TELLER
TOM WILSON & TOM II

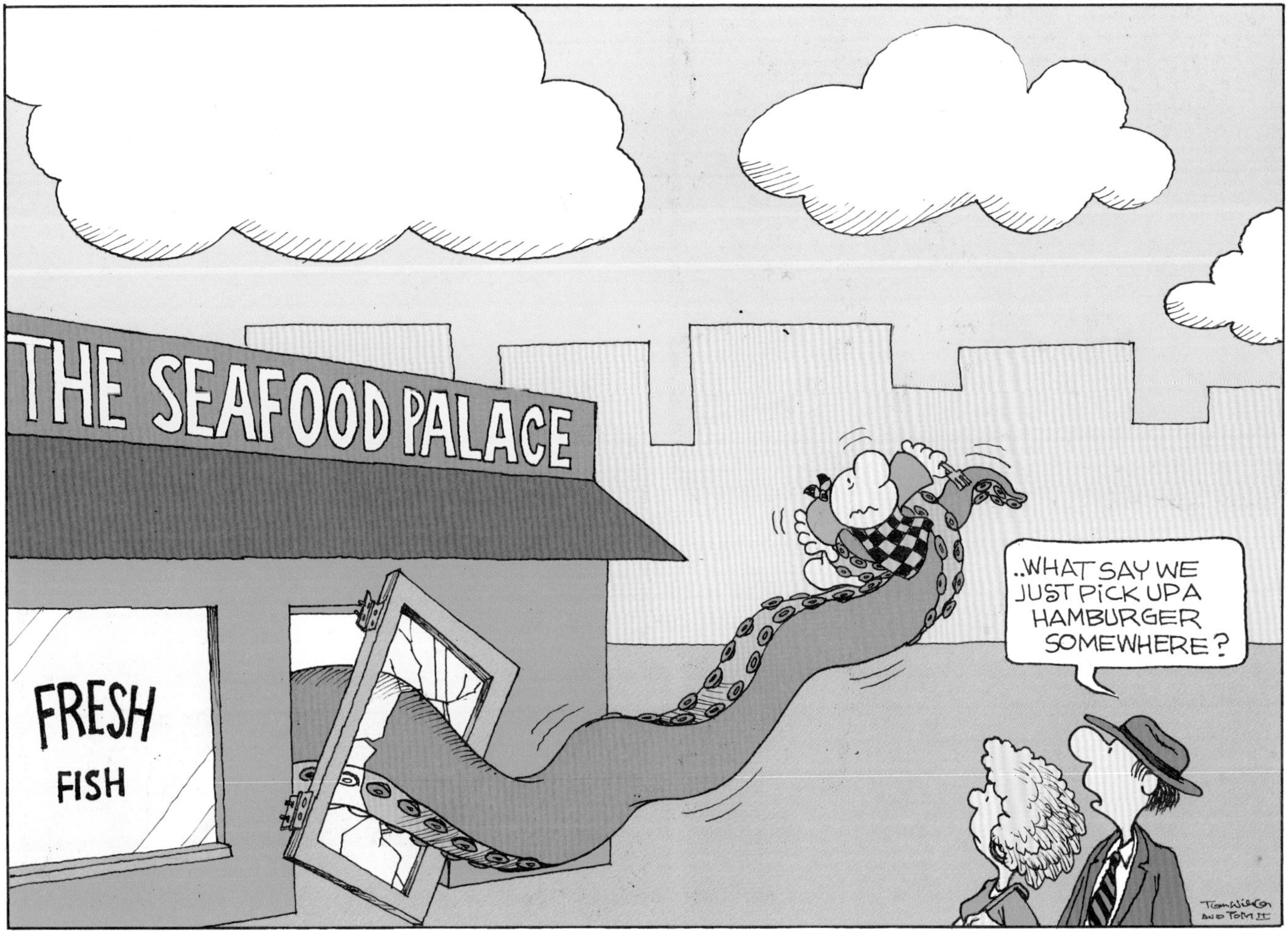
THE SEAFOOD PALACE
FRESH
FISH
..WHAT SAY WE JUST PICK UP A HAMBURGER SOMEWHERE?

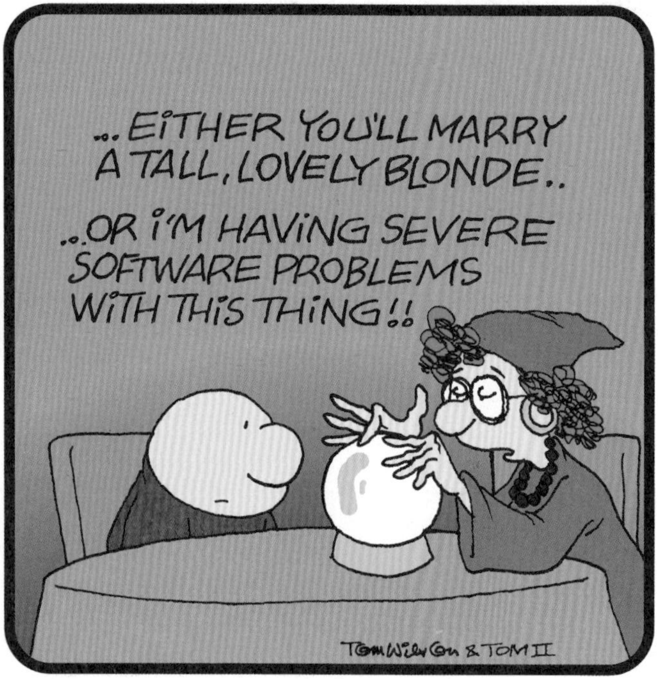
...EITHER YOU'LL MARRY A TALL, LOVELY BLONDE..
..OR I'M HAVING SEVERE SOFTWARE PROBLEMS WITH THIS THING!!
TOM WILSON & TOM II

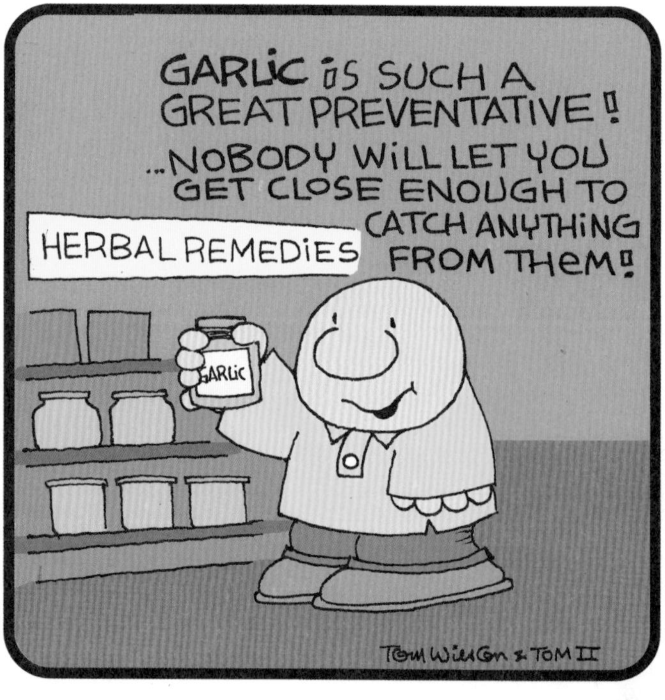
GARLIC IS SUCH A GREAT PREVENTATIVE! ...NOBODY WILL LET YOU GET CLOSE ENOUGH TO CATCH ANYTHING FROM THEM!
HERBAL REMEDIES
GARLIC
TOM WILSON & TOM II

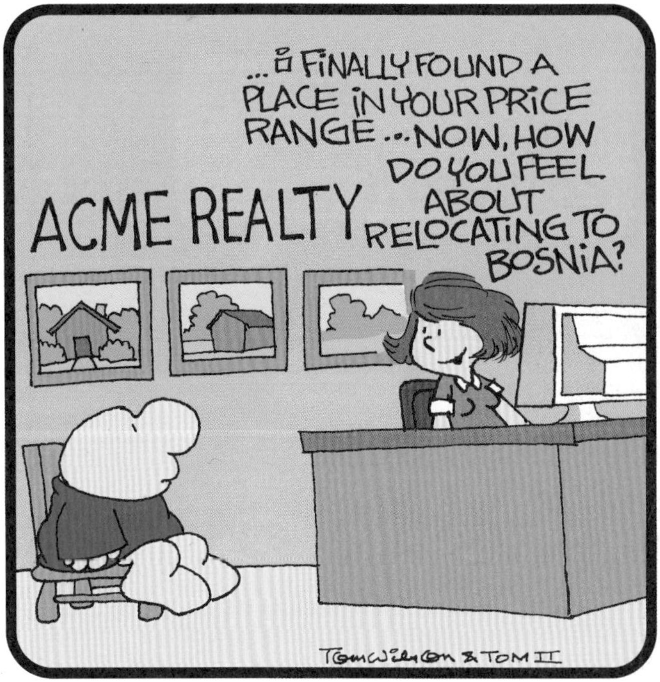
...I FINALLY FOUND A PLACE IN YOUR PRICE RANGE...NOW, HOW DO YOU FEEL ABOUT RELOCATING TO BOSNIA?
ACME REALTY
TOM WILSON & TOM II

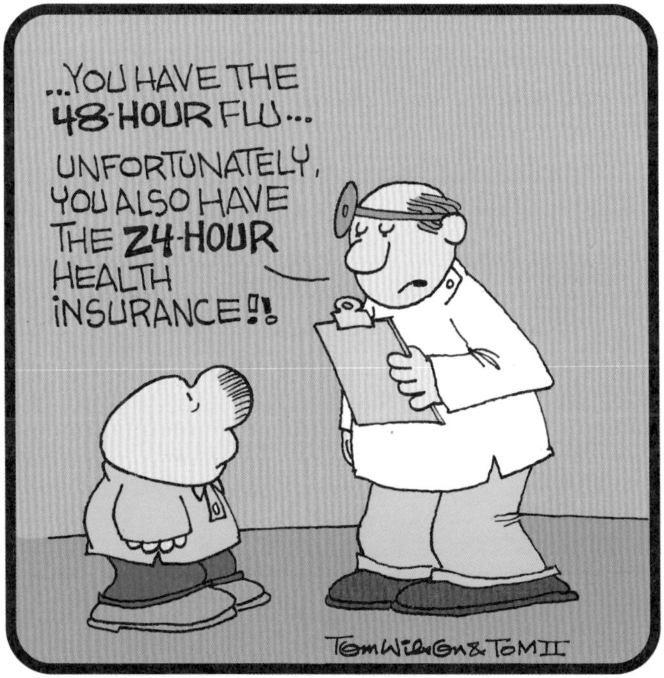
...YOU HAVE THE 48-HOUR FLU...
UNFORTUNATELY, YOU ALSO HAVE THE 24-HOUR HEALTH INSURANCE!!
TOM WILSON & TOM II

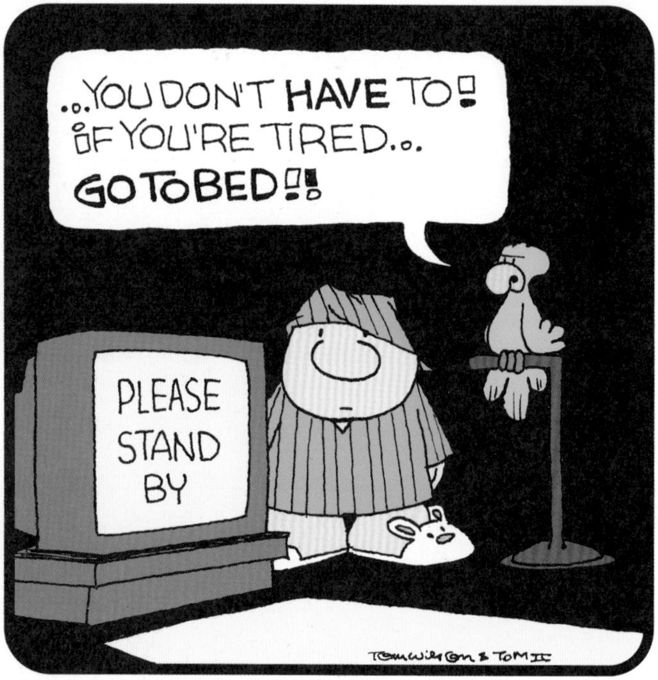
..YOU DON'T HAVE TO!
IF YOU'RE TIRED..
GO TO BED!!
PLEASE STAND BY
TOM WILSON & TOM II

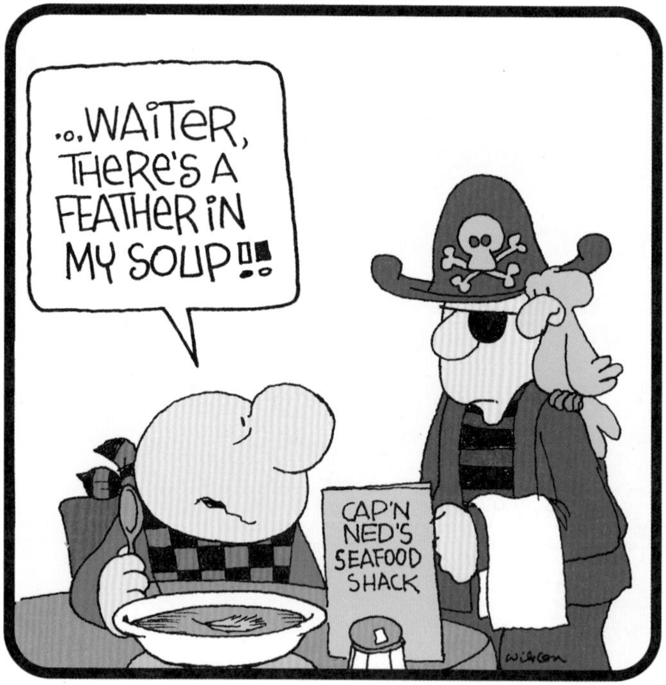
..WAITER, THERE'S A FEATHER IN MY SOUP!!
CAP'N NED'S SEAFOOD SHACK
WILSON

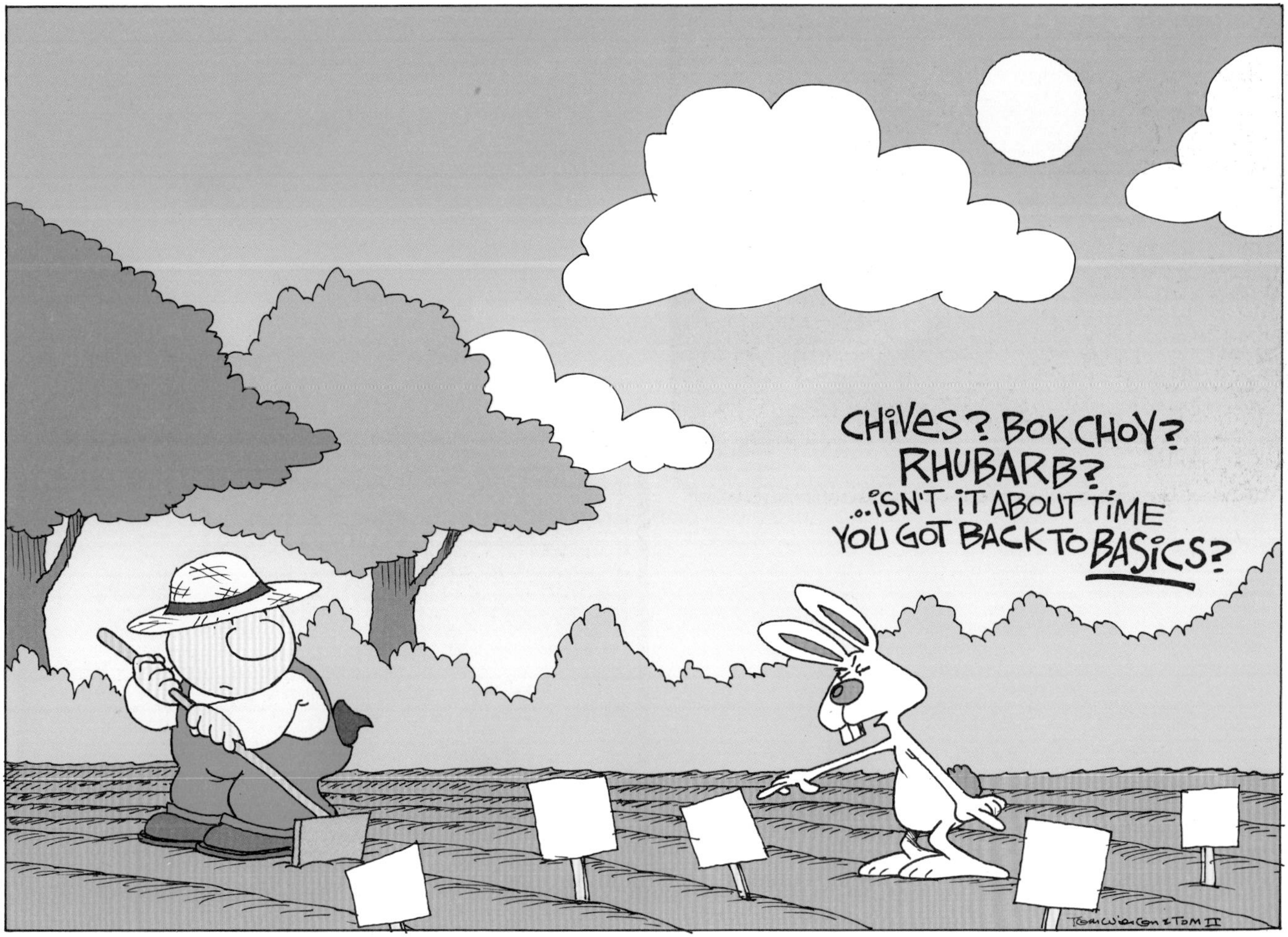
CHIVES? BOK CHOY? RHUBARB? ...ISN'T IT ABOUT TIME YOU GOT BACK TO BASICS?
TOM WILSON & TOM II

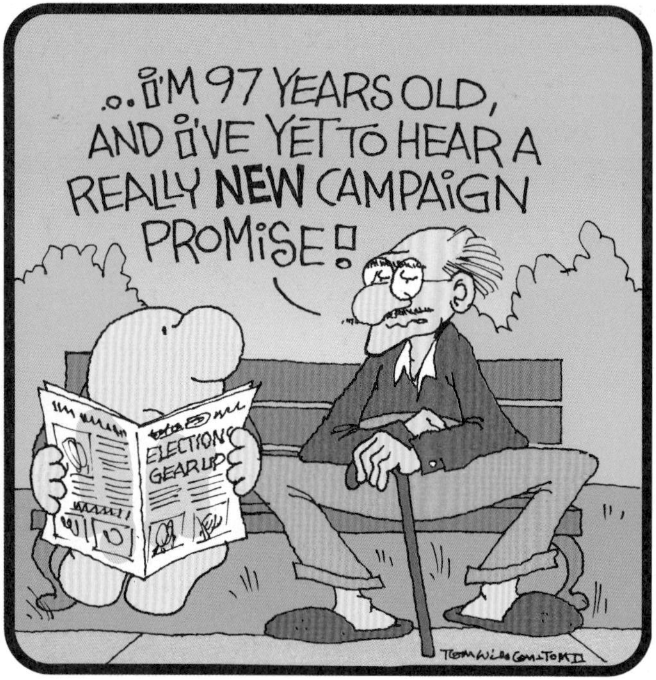
..I'M 97 YEARS OLD, AND I'VE YET TO HEAR A REALLY NEW CAMPAIGN PROMISE!
ELECTION GEAR UP

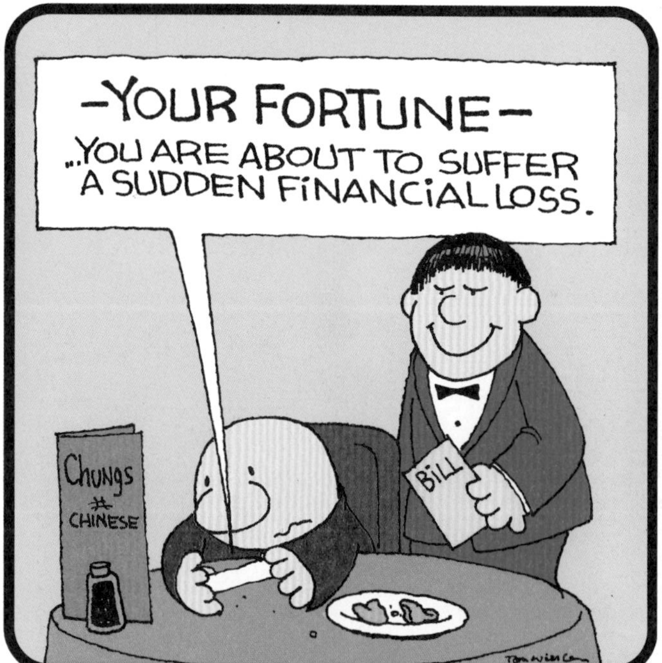
-YOUR FORTUNE-
..YOU ARE ABOUT TO SUFFER A SUDDEN FINANCIAL LOSS.
Chungs
CHINESE
BILL

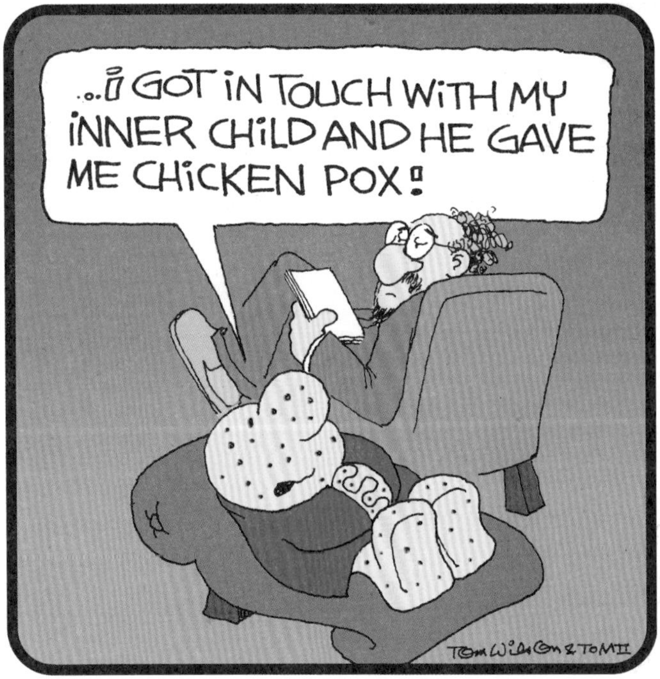
...I GOT IN TOUCH WITH MY INNER CHILD AND HE GAVE ME CHICKEN POX!
TOM WILSON & TOM II

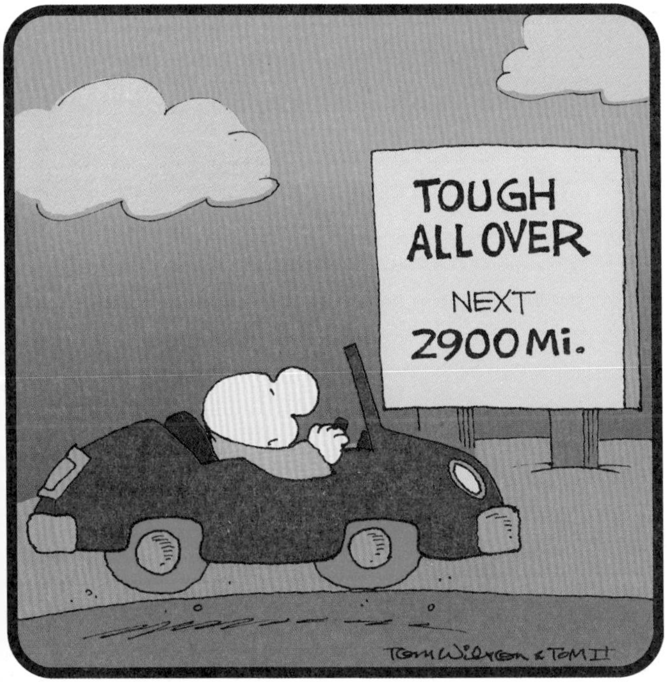
TOUGH ALL OVER
NEXT
2900 Mi.
TOM WILSON & TOM II

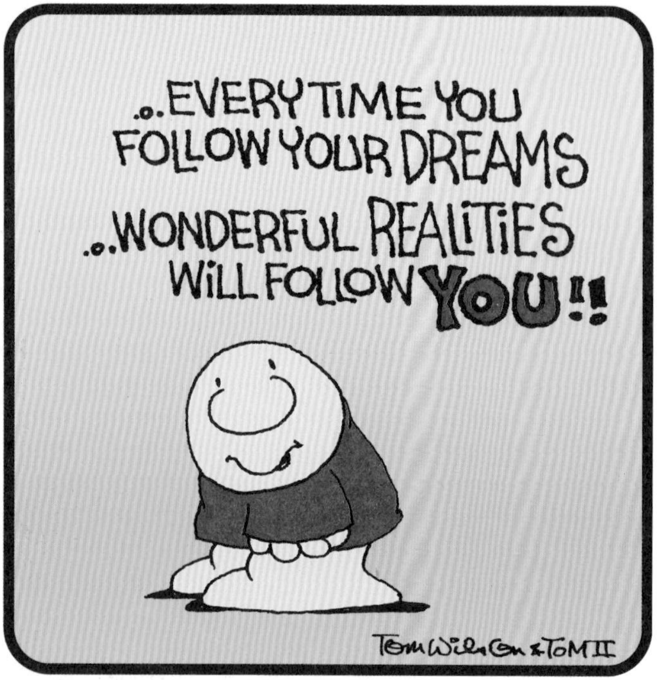
..EVERY TIME YOU FOLLOW YOUR DREAMS
..WONDERFUL REALITIES WILL FOLLOW YOU!!
Tom Wilson & Tom II

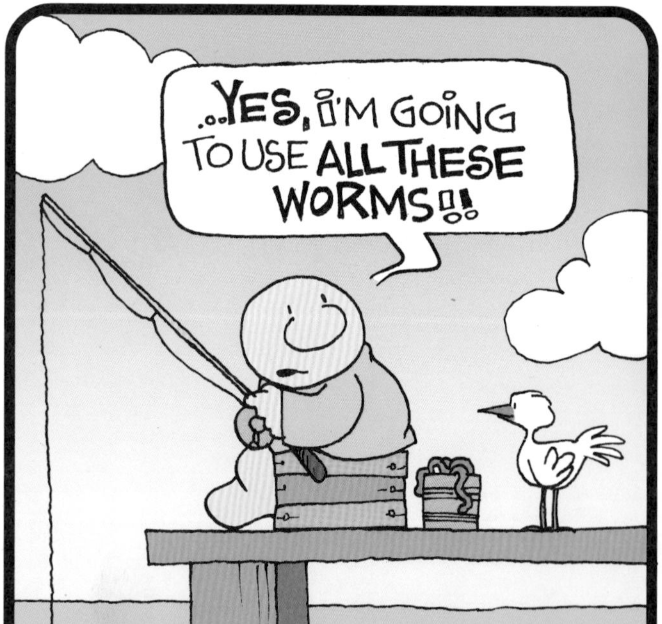
..YES, I'M GOING TO USE ALL THESE WORMS!!
Tom Wilson & Tom II

..DO YOU REALIZE THAT WE'VE BEEN OUT HERE FOR 3 HOURS AND YOU HAVEN'T HAD A SINGLE BITE?
..THAT'S BECAUSE I'M NOT USING ANY BAIT!!
HUH?
...SOMETIMES IT'S THE FISH I'M AFTER...
...AND SOMETIMES IT'S JUST THE FISHING!
TOM WILSON & TOM II

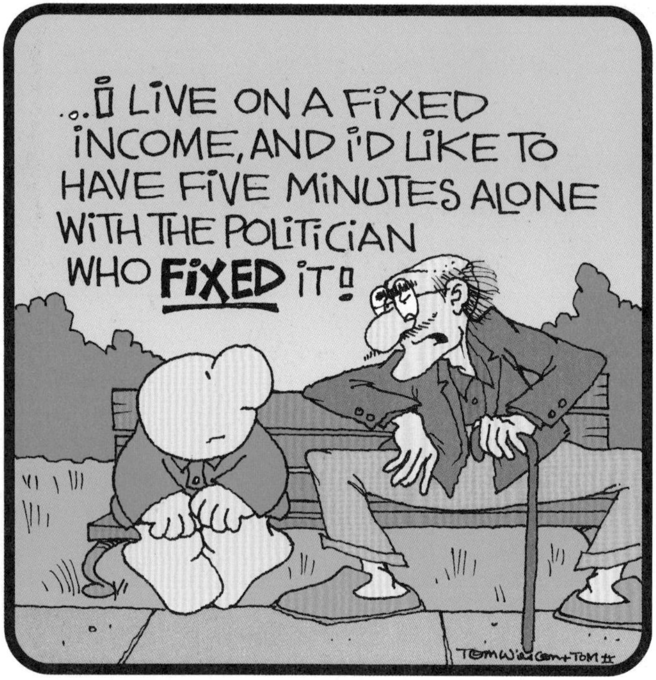
..I LIVE ON A FIXED INCOME, AND I'D LIKE TO HAVE FIVE MINUTES ALONE WITH THE POLITICIAN WHO **FIXED** IT!!

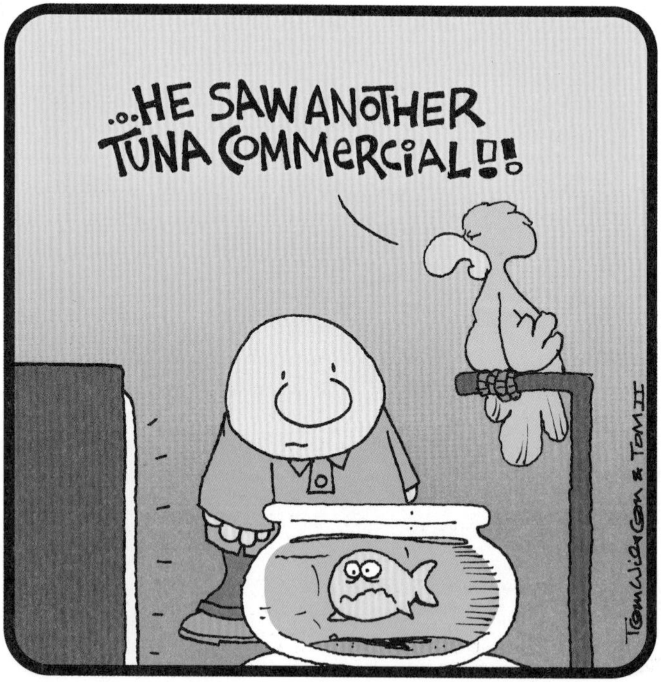
..HE SAW ANOTHER TUNA COMMERCIAL!!!

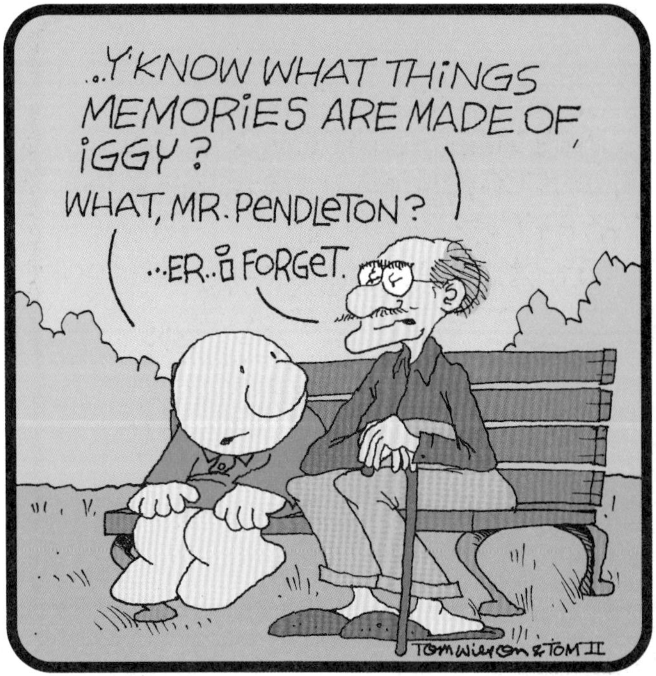
..Y'KNOW WHAT THINGS MEMORIES ARE MADE OF, IGGY?
WHAT, MR. PENDLETON?
...ER.. I FORGET.
TOM WILSON & TOM II

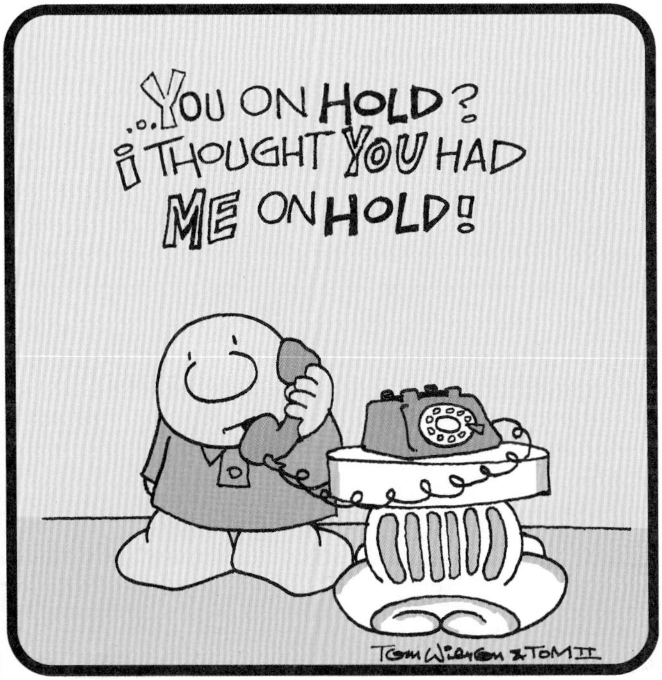
...YOU ON HOLD? I THOUGHT YOU HAD ME ON HOLD!
TOM WILSON & TOM II

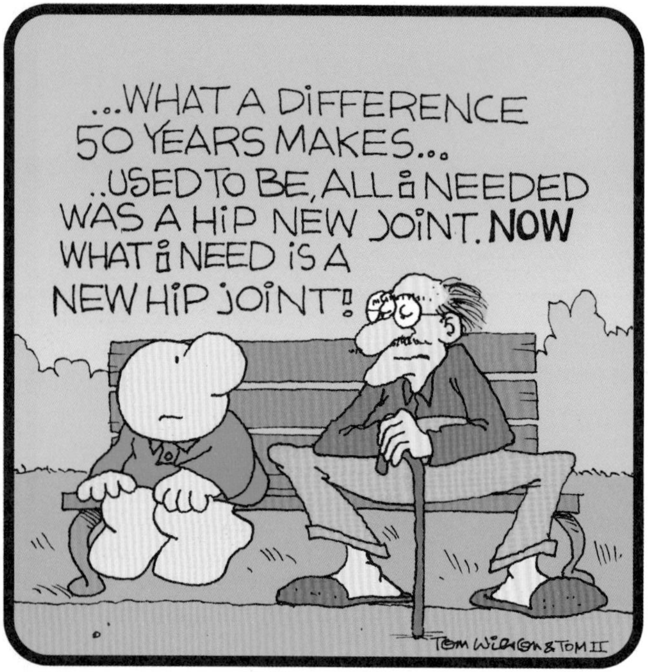
...WHAT A DIFFERENCE 50 YEARS MAKES... ..USED TO BE, ALL I NEEDED WAS A HIP NEW JOINT. NOW WHAT I NEED IS A NEW HIP JOINT!
TOM WILSON & TOM II

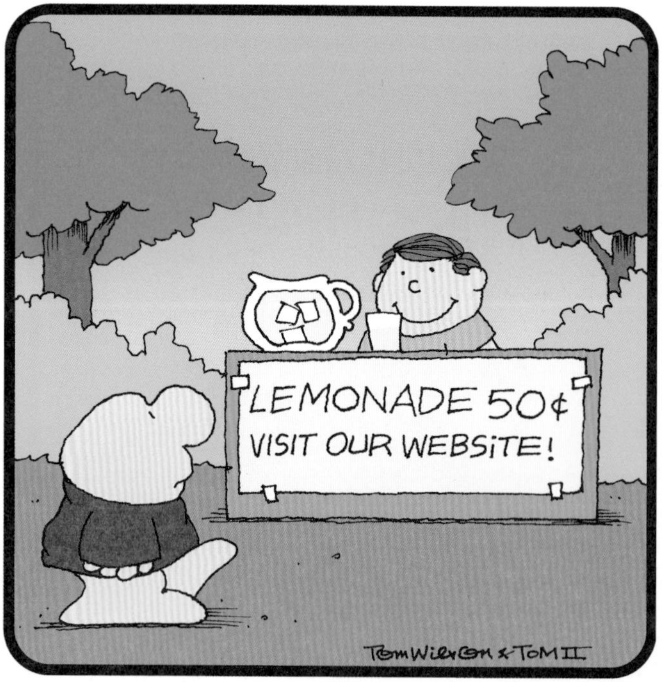
LEMONADE 50¢
VISIT OUR WEBSITE!
TOM WILSON & TOM II

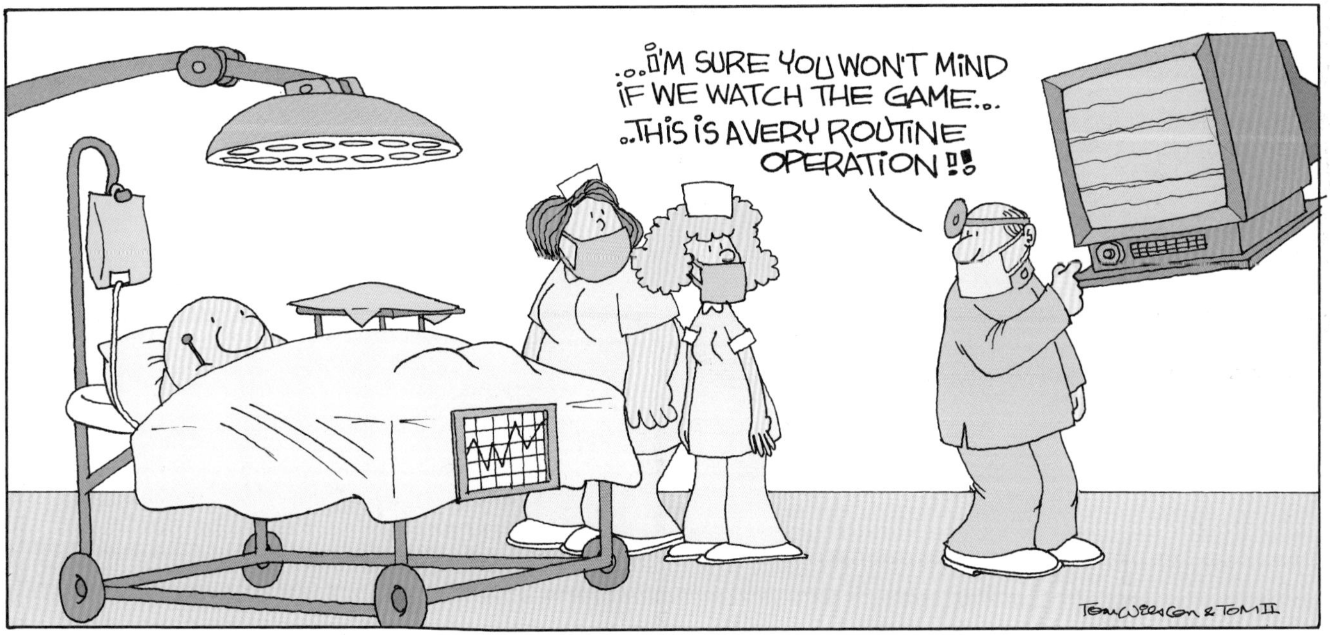
...I'M SURE YOU WON'T MIND IF WE WATCH THE GAME... ..THIS IS A VERY ROUTINE OPERATION!!
TOM WILSON & TOM II

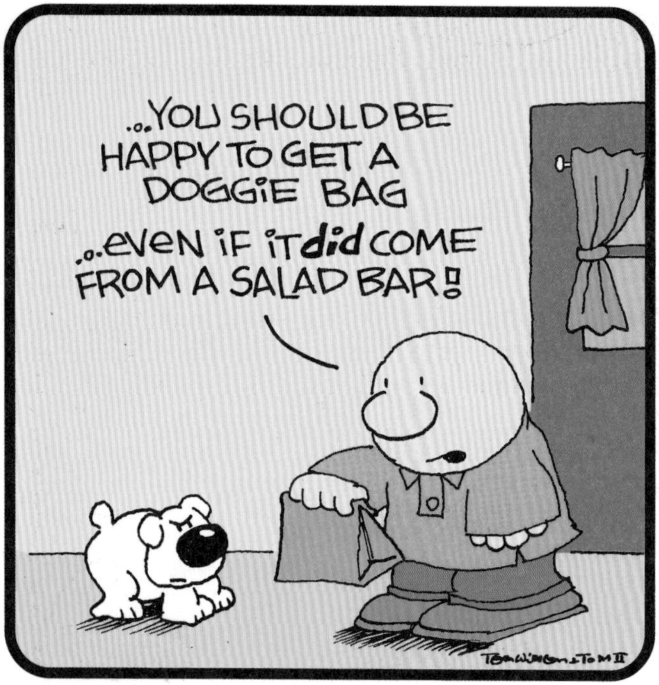
..YOU SHOULD BE HAPPY TO GET A DOGGIE BAG ..even IF IT *did* COME FROM A SALAD BAR!
TOM WILSON + TOM II

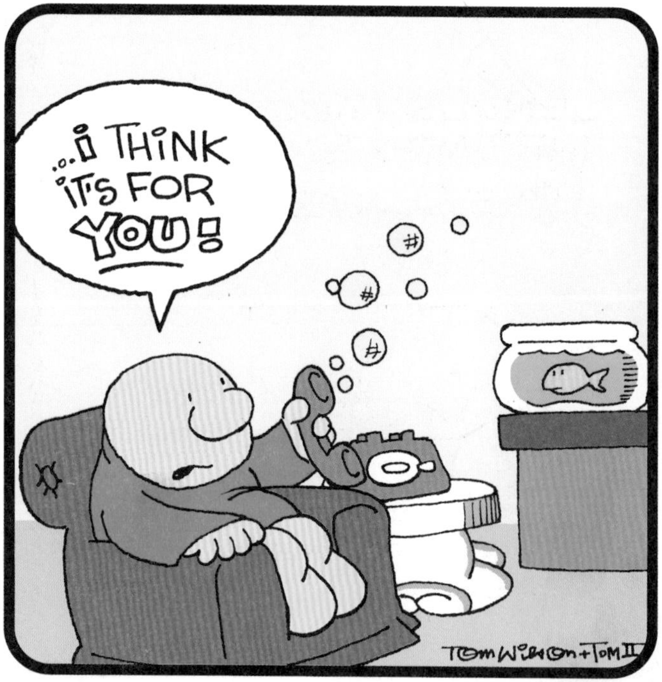
..I THINK IT'S FOR YOU!
TOM WILSON + TOM II

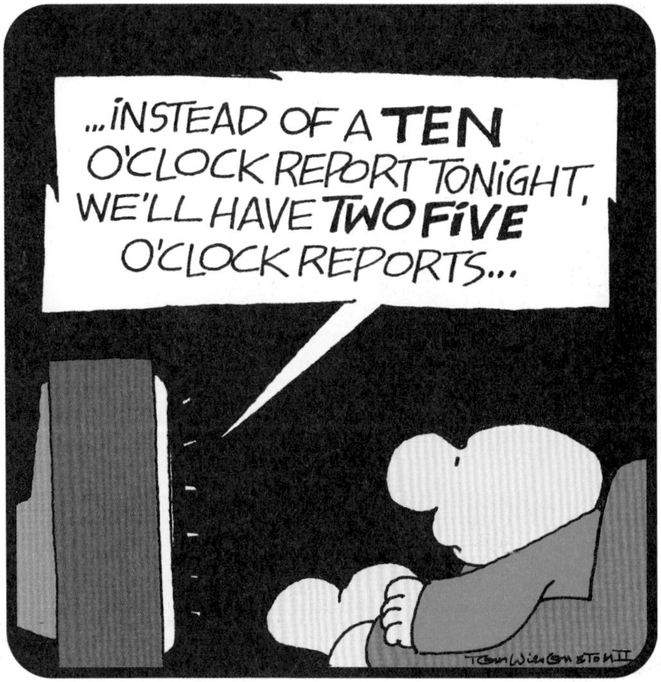
...INSTEAD OF A TEN O'CLOCK REPORT TONIGHT, WE'LL HAVE TWO FIVE O'CLOCK REPORTS...
Tom Wilson & Tom II

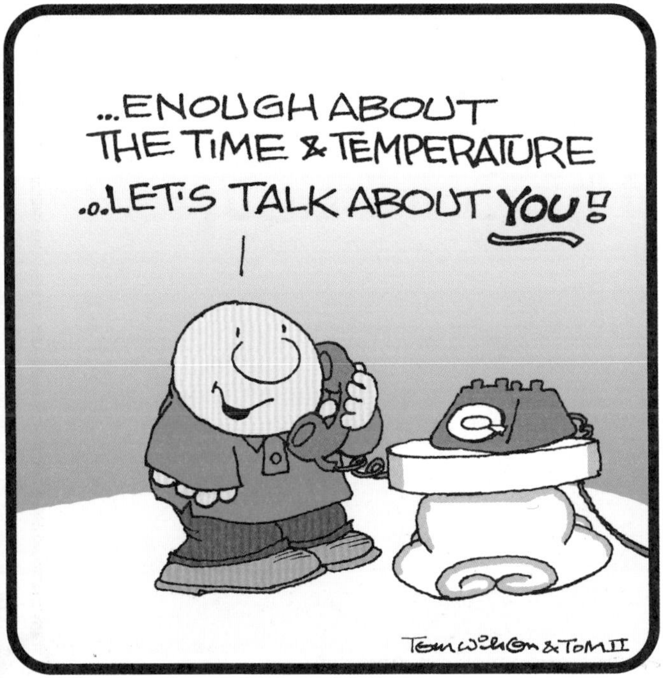
...ENOUGH ABOUT THE TIME & TEMPERATURE ...LET'S TALK ABOUT YOU!!
Tom Wilson & Tom II

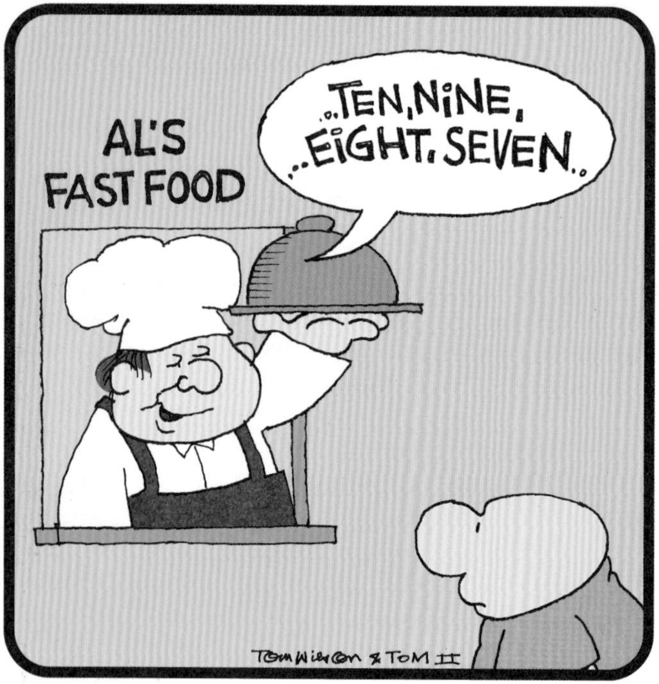
AL'S
FAST FOOD
...TEN, NINE, ...EIGHT, SEVEN...
TOM WILSON & TOM II

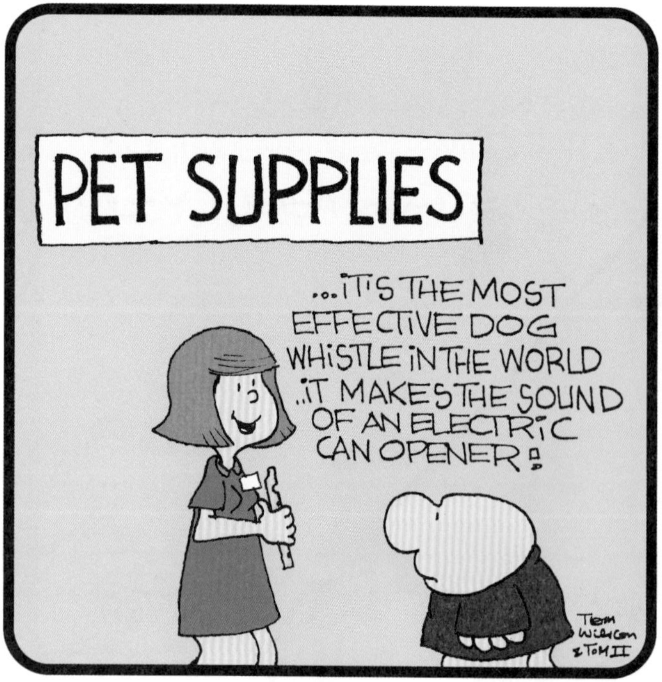
PET SUPPLIES
...IT'S THE MOST EFFECTIVE DOG WHISTLE IN THE WORLD ..IT MAKES THE SOUND OF AN ELECTRIC CAN OPENER!
TOM WILSON & TOM II

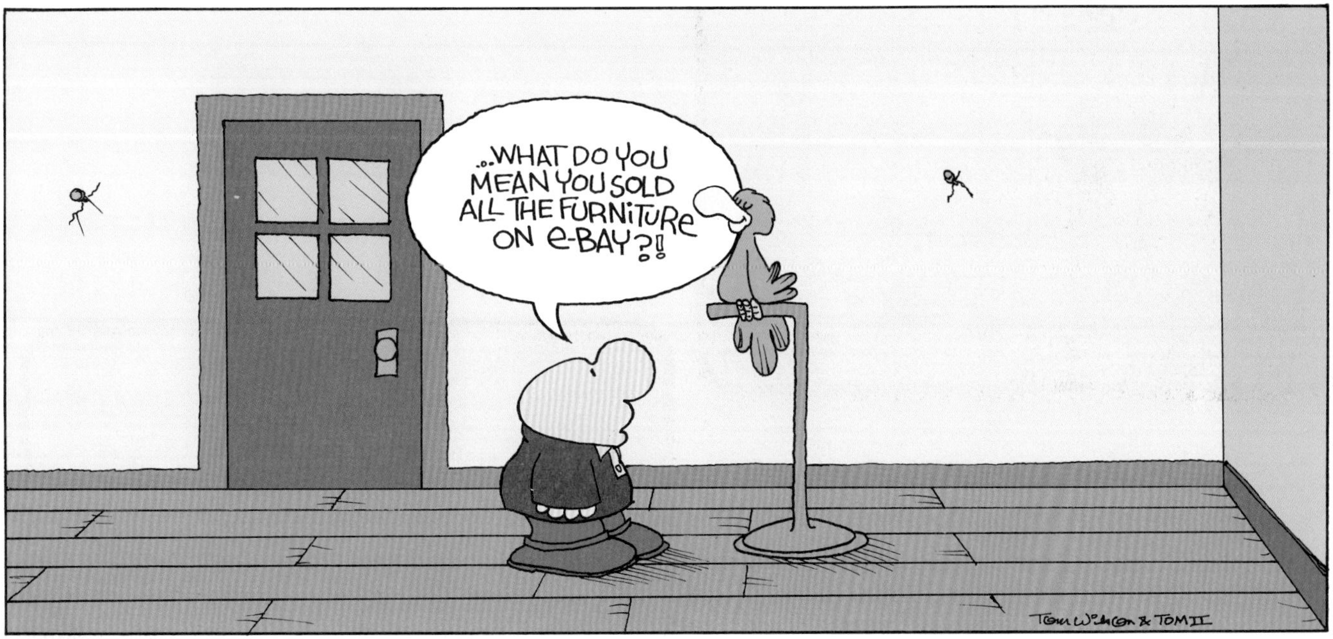
..WHAT DO YOU MEAN YOU SOLD ALL THE FURNITURE ON e-BAY?!
TOM WILSON & TOM II

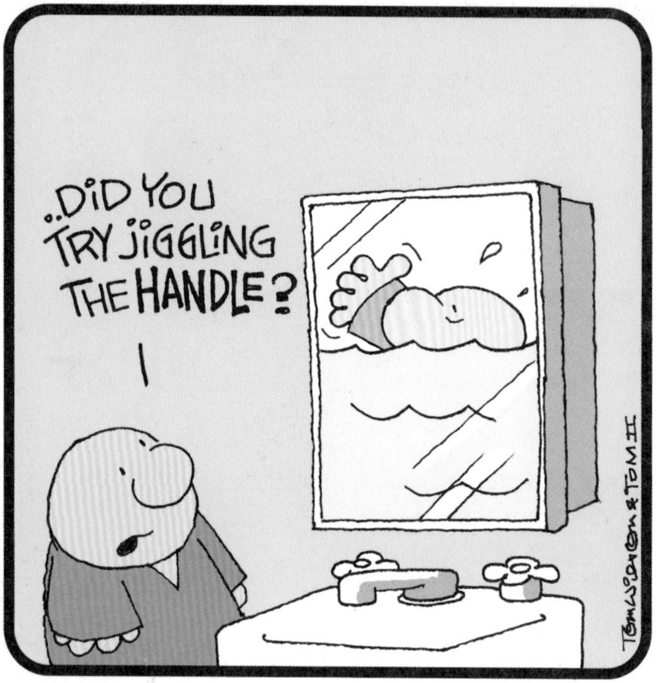
..DID YOU TRY JIGGLING THE HANDLE?
TOM WILSON & TOM II

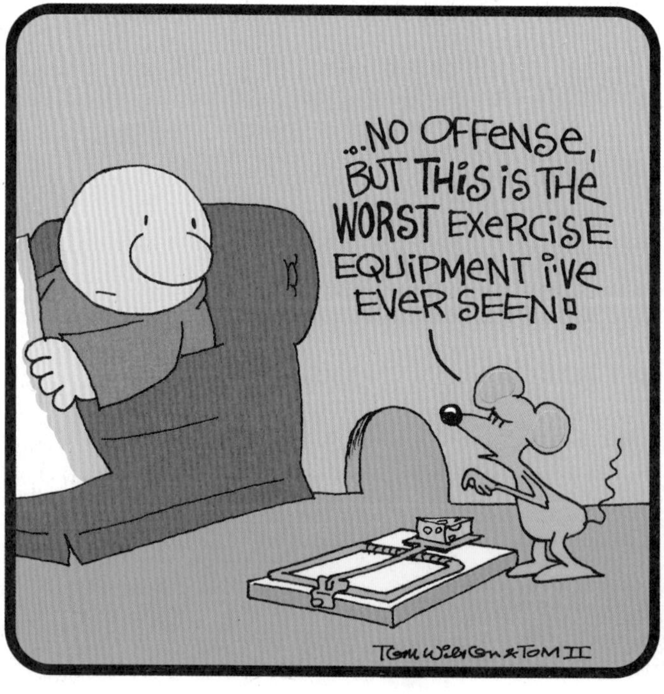
..NO OFFENSE, BUT THIS IS THE WORST EXERCISE EQUIPMENT I'VE EVER SEEN!
TOM WILSON & TOM II

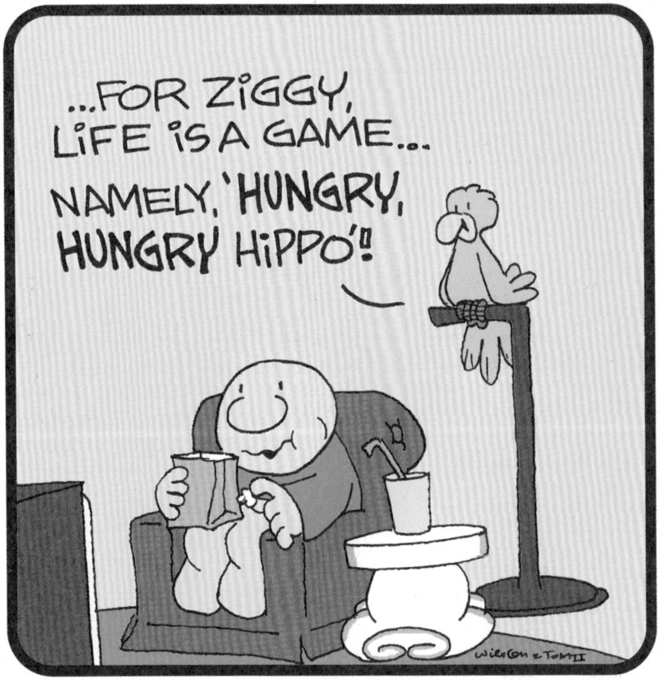
...FOR ZIGGY, LIFE IS A GAME...
NAMELY, 'HUNGRY, HUNGRY HIPPO'!!
WILSON & TOM II

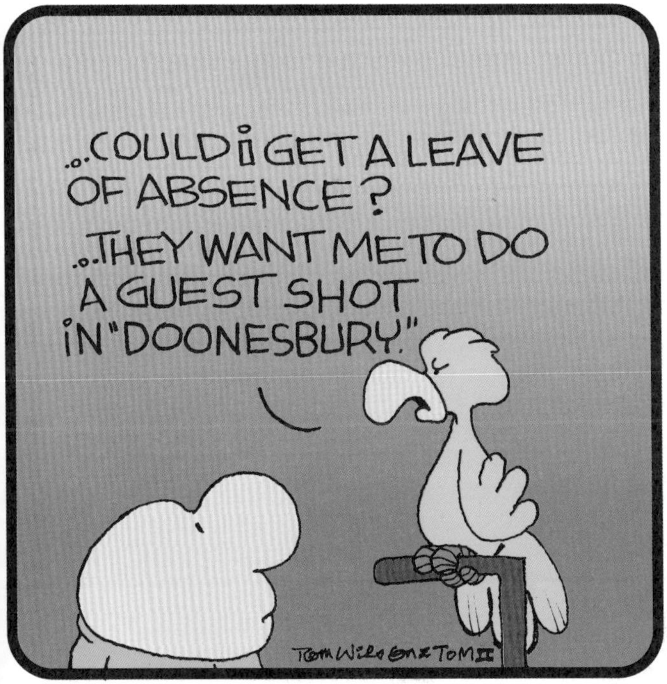
...COULD I GET A LEAVE OF ABSENCE?
...THEY WANT ME TO DO A GUEST SHOT IN "DOONESBURY."
TOM WILSON & TOM II

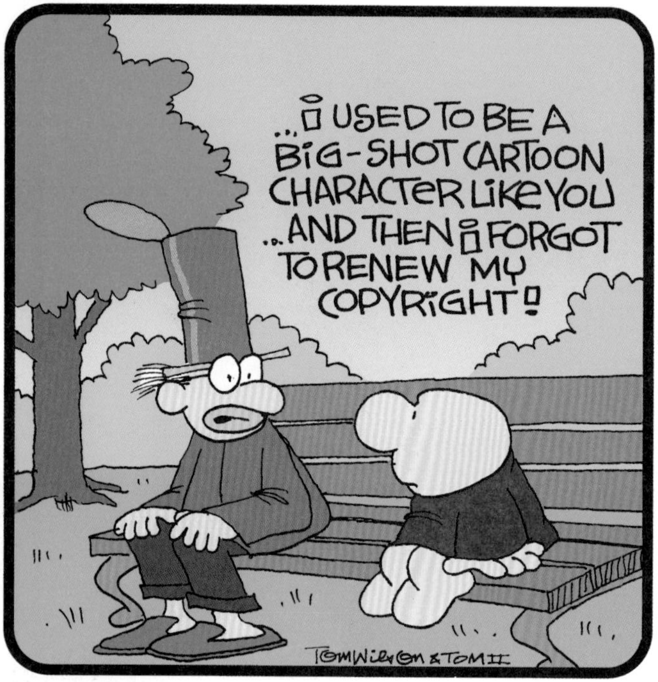
...I USED TO BE A BIG-SHOT CARTOON CHARACTER LIKE YOU ...AND THEN I FORGOT TO RENEW MY COPYRIGHT!
TOM WILSON & TOM II

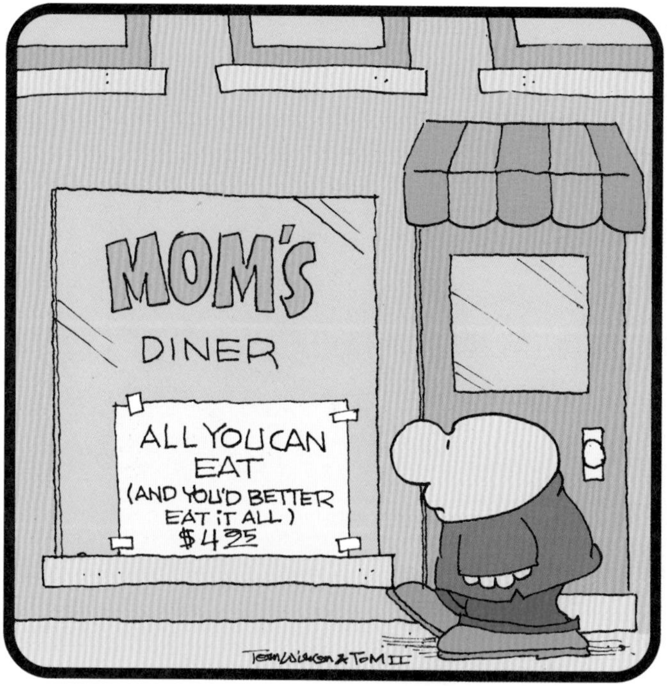
MOM'S
DINER
ALL YOU CAN EAT
(AND YOU'D BETTER EAT IT ALL)
$4.25
TOM WILSON & TOM II

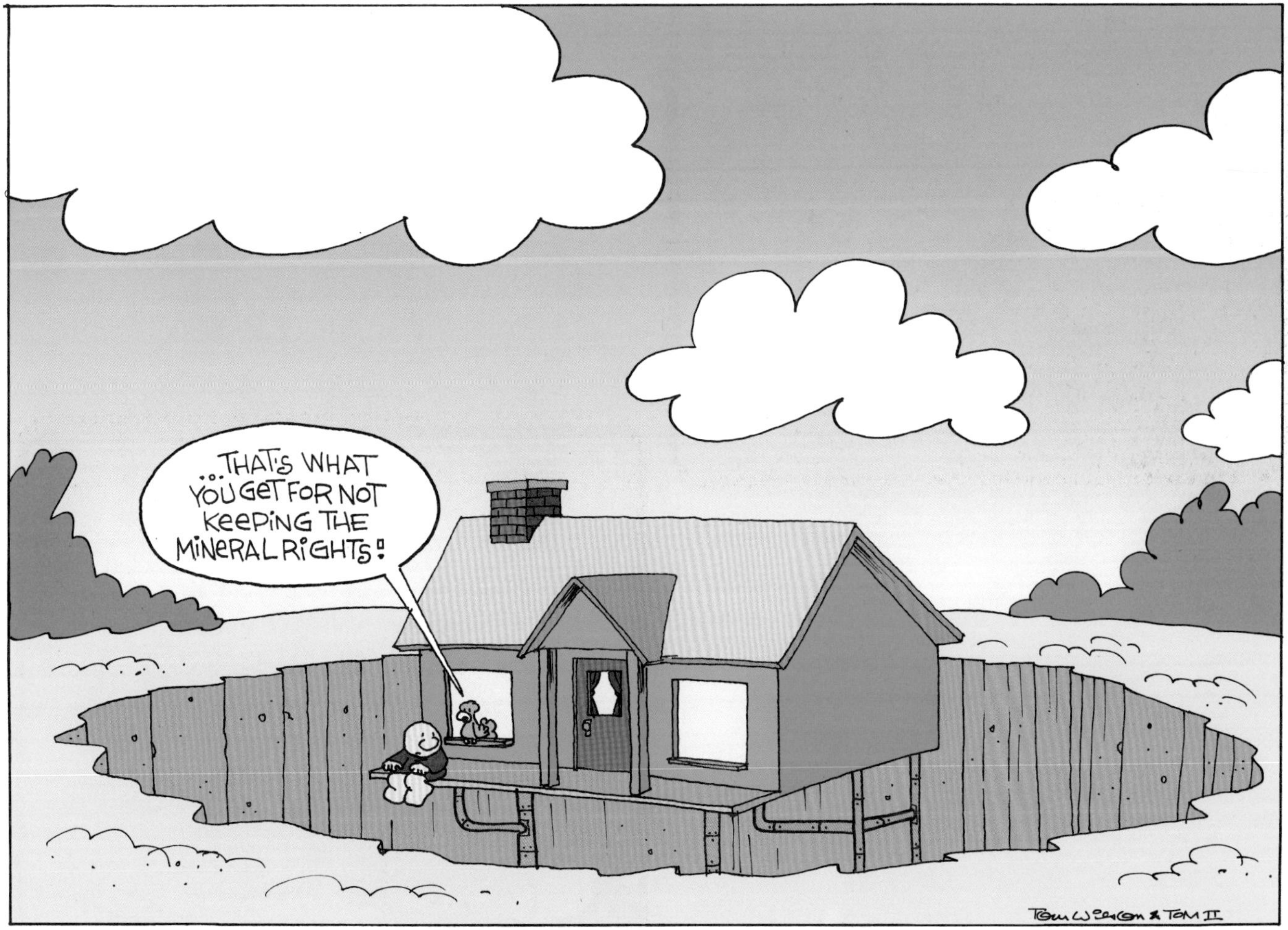
...THAT'S WHAT YOU GET FOR NOT KEEPING THE MINERAL RIGHTS!
TOM WILSON & TOM II

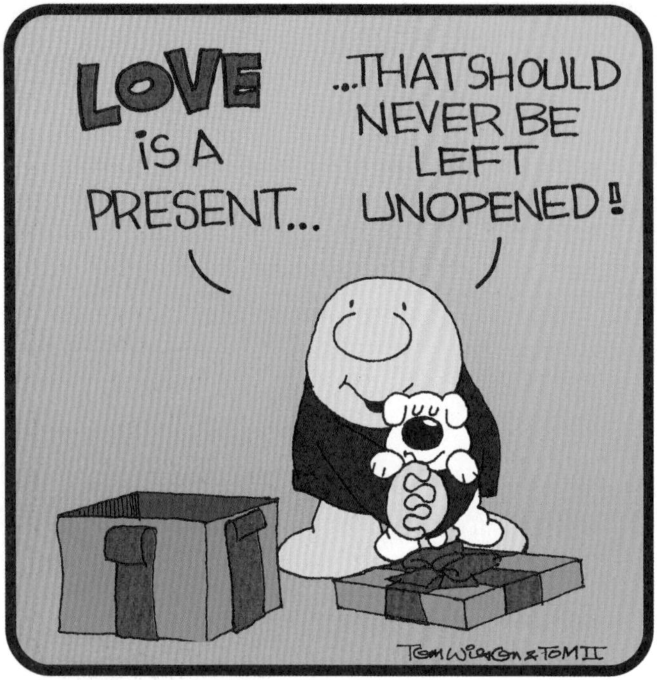
LOVE is A PRESENT...
...THAT SHOULD NEVER BE LEFT UNOPENED!
TOM WILSON & TOM II

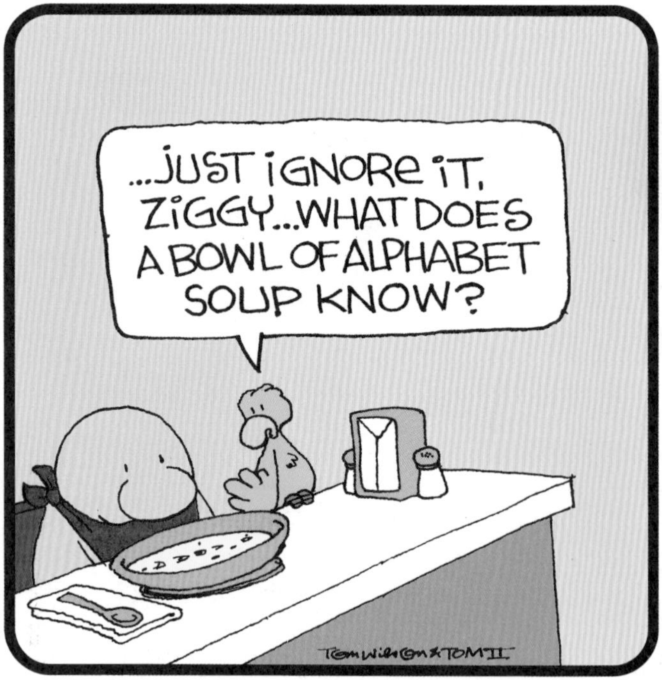
...JUST iGNORE iT, ZiGGY...WHAT DOES A BOWL OF ALPHABET SOUP KNOW?
TOM WILSON & TOM II

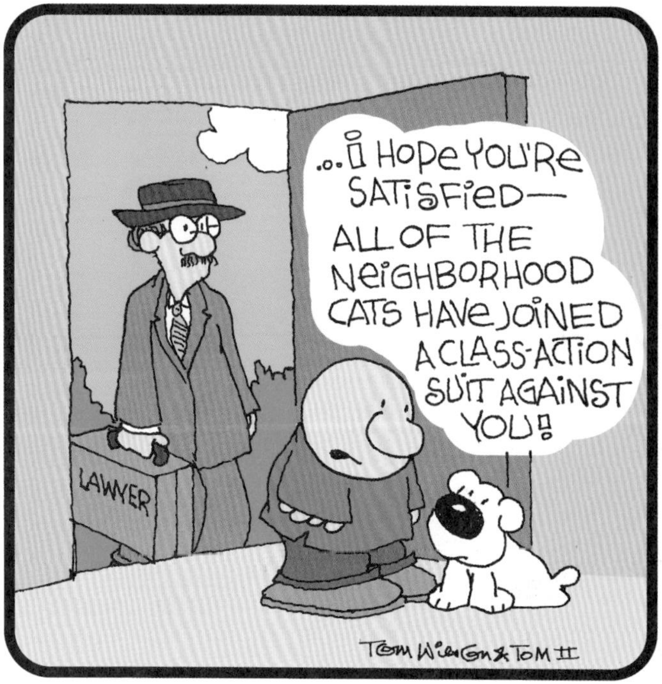
...I HOPE YOU'RE SATISFIED— ALL OF THE NEIGHBORHOOD CATS HAVE JOINED A CLASS-ACTION SUIT AGAINST YOU!
LAWYER
Tom Wilson & Tom II

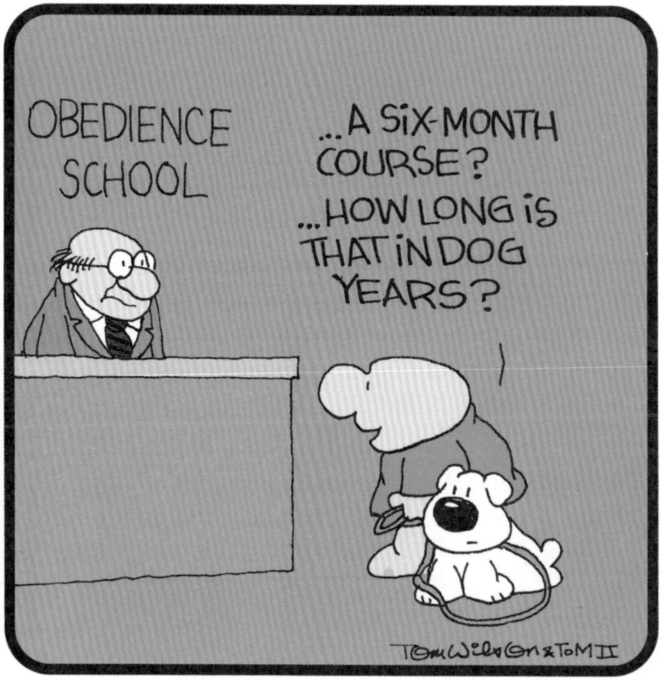
OBEDIENCE SCHOOL
...A SIX-MONTH COURSE? ...HOW LONG IS THAT IN DOG YEARS?
Tom Wilson & Tom II

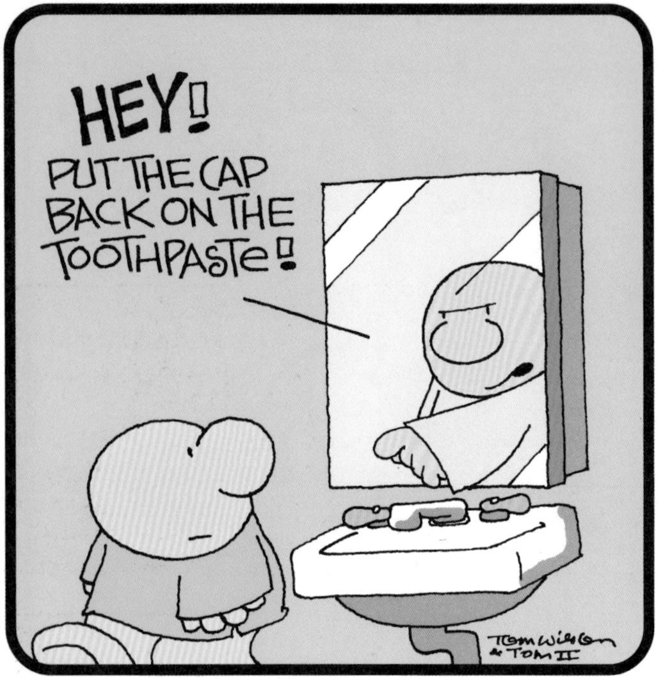
HEY!!
PUT THE CAP BACK ON THE TOOTHPASTE!!
Tom Wilson & Tom II

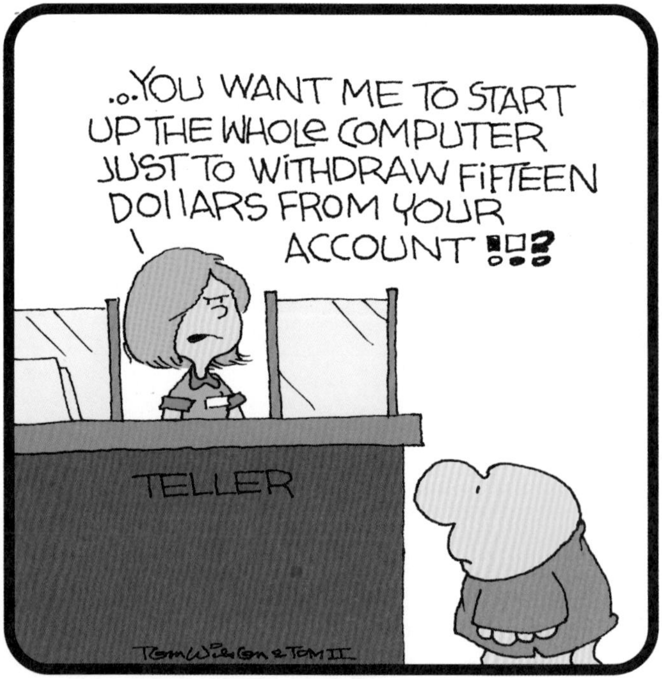
...YOU WANT ME TO START UP THE WHOLE COMPUTER JUST TO WITHDRAW FIFTEEN DOLLARS FROM YOUR ACCOUNT!!?
TELLER
Tom Wilson & Tom II

POP!
FOOSH!!
...THANKS. BUT NEXT TIME, LET ME OPEN MY OWN POTATO CHIP BAG!
TOM WILSON & TOM II

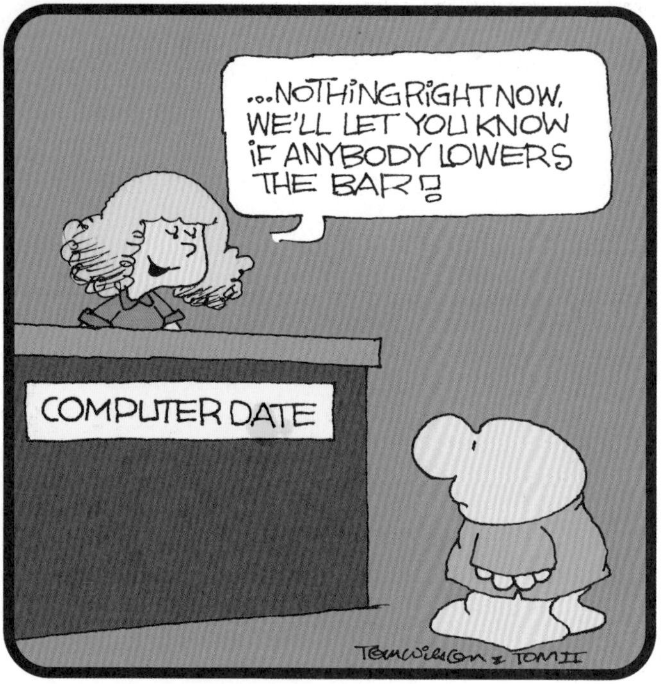
...NOTHING RIGHT NOW. WE'LL LET YOU KNOW IF ANYBODY LOWERS THE BAR!!
COMPUTER DATE
TOM WILSON & TOM II

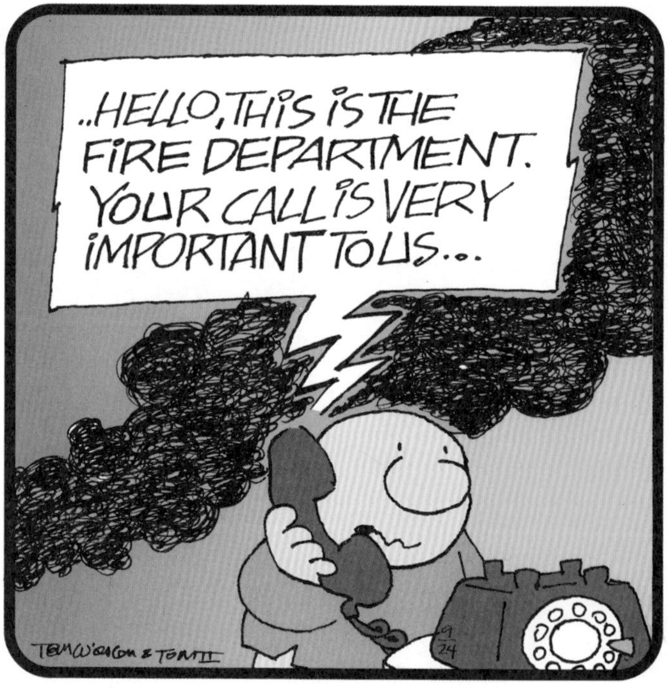
..HELLO, THIS IS THE FIRE DEPARTMENT. YOUR CALL IS VERY IMPORTANT TO US...
TOM WILSON & TOM II
9/24

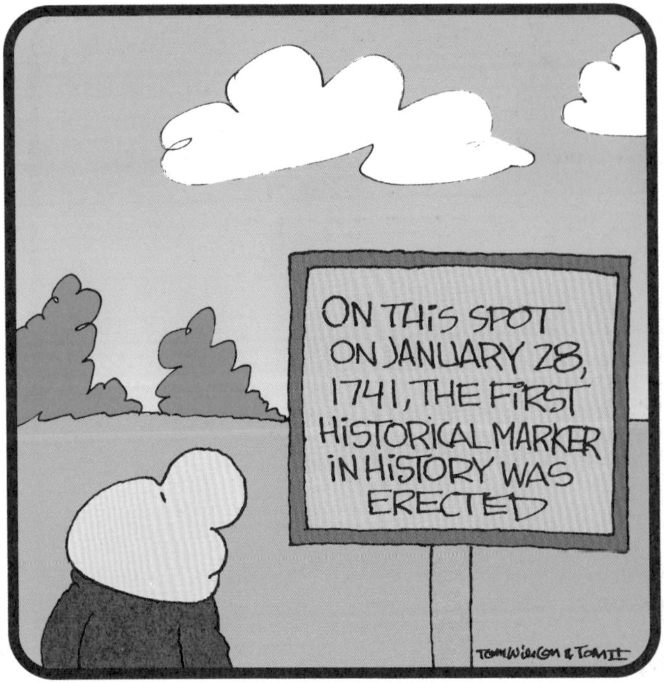
ON THIS SPOT ON JANUARY 28, 1741, THE FIRST HISTORICAL MARKER IN HISTORY WAS ERECTED
TOM WILSON & TOM II

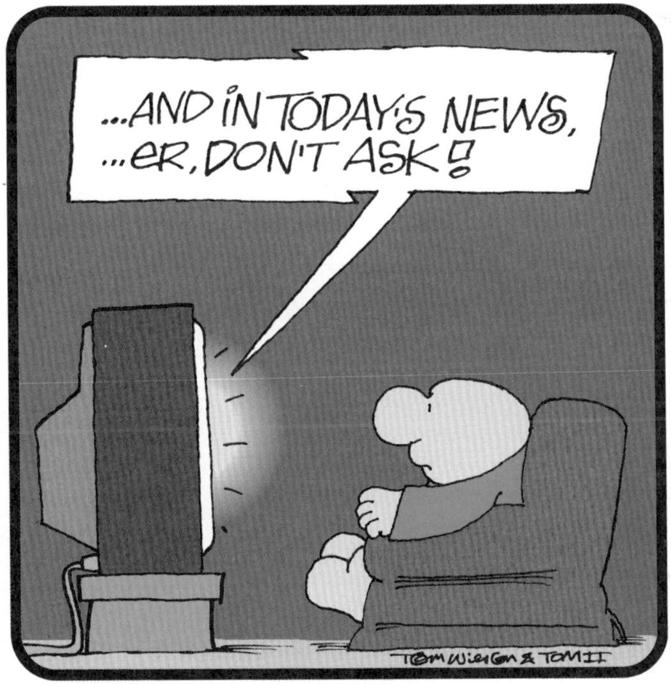
...AND IN TODAY'S NEWS, ...ER, DON'T ASK!!
TOM WILSON & TOM II

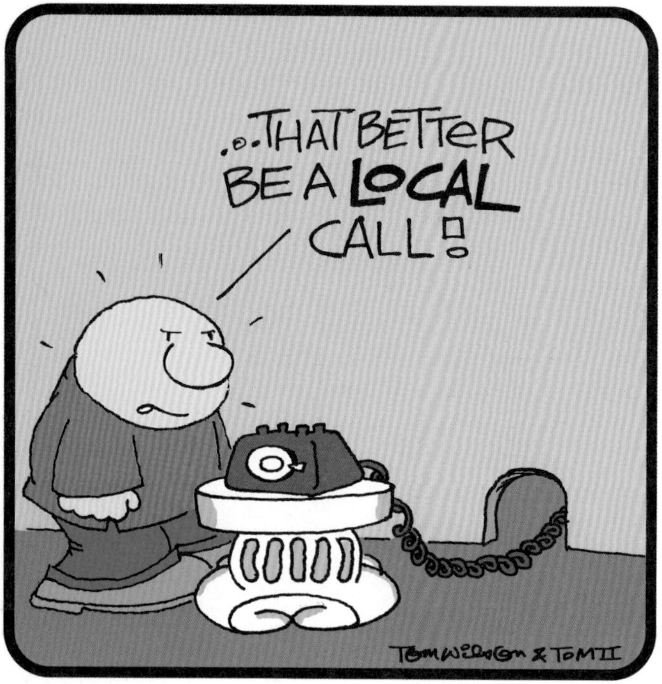
..THAT BETTER BE A LOCAL CALL!
TOM WILSON & TOM II

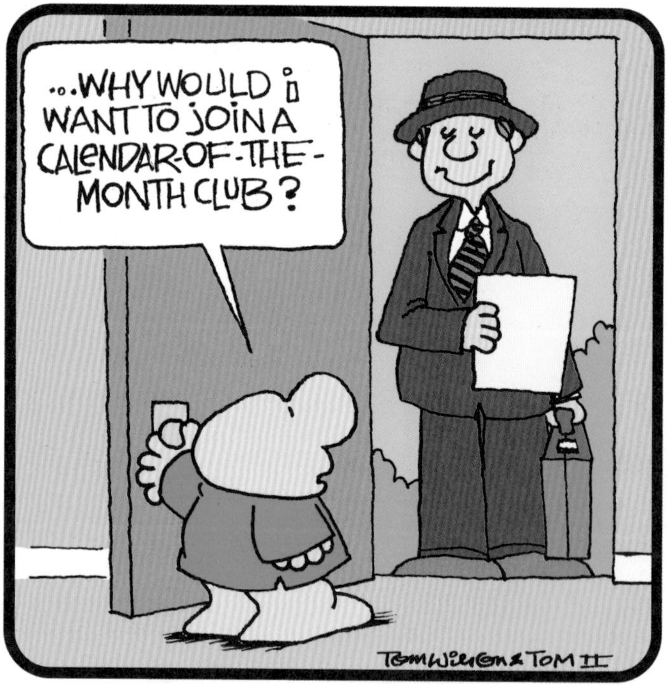
..WHY WOULD I WANT TO JOIN A CALENDAR-OF-THE-MONTH CLUB?
TOM WILSON & TOM II

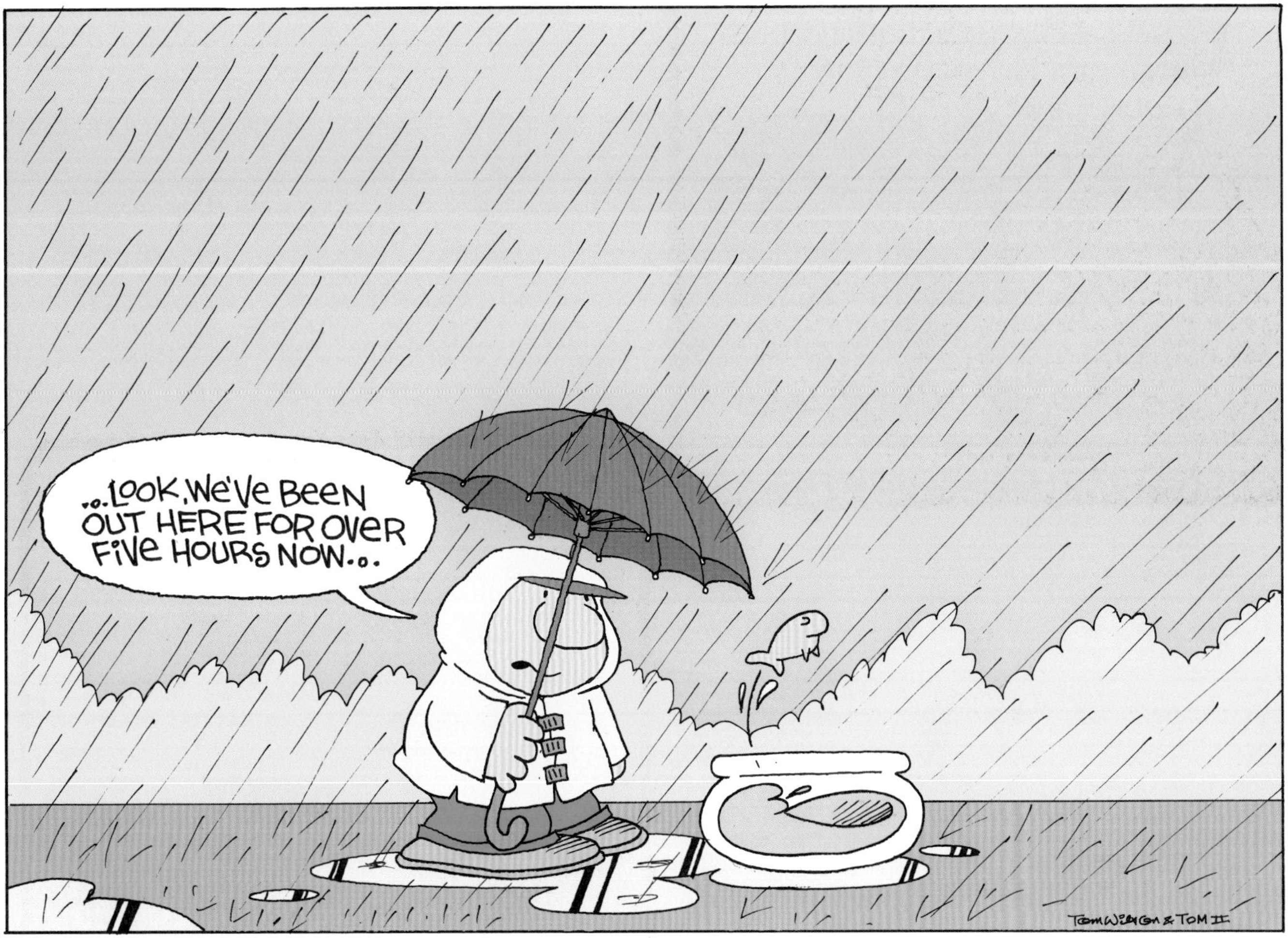
..LOOK, WE'VE BEEN OUT HERE FOR OVER FIVE HOURS NOW...
TOM WILSON & TOM II

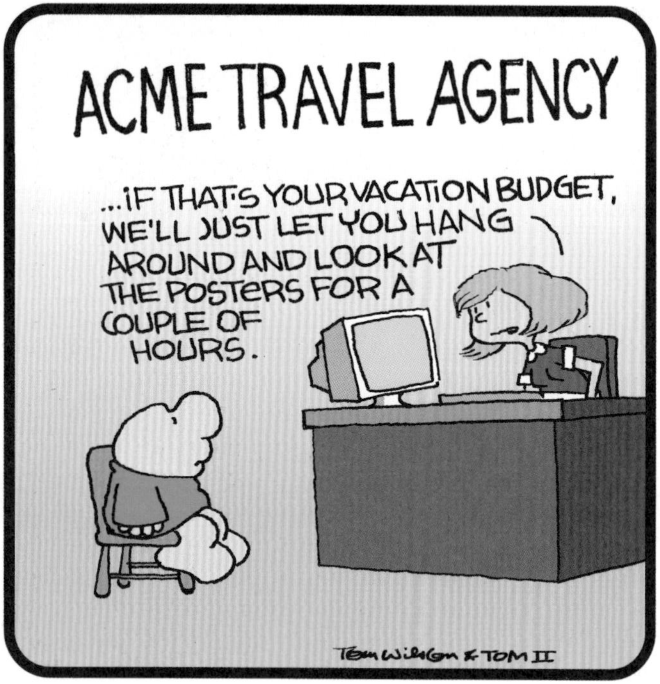
ACME TRAVEL AGENCY
...IF THAT'S YOUR VACATION BUDGET, WE'LL JUST LET YOU HANG AROUND AND LOOK AT THE POSTERS FOR A COUPLE OF HOURS.
Tom Wilson & TOM II

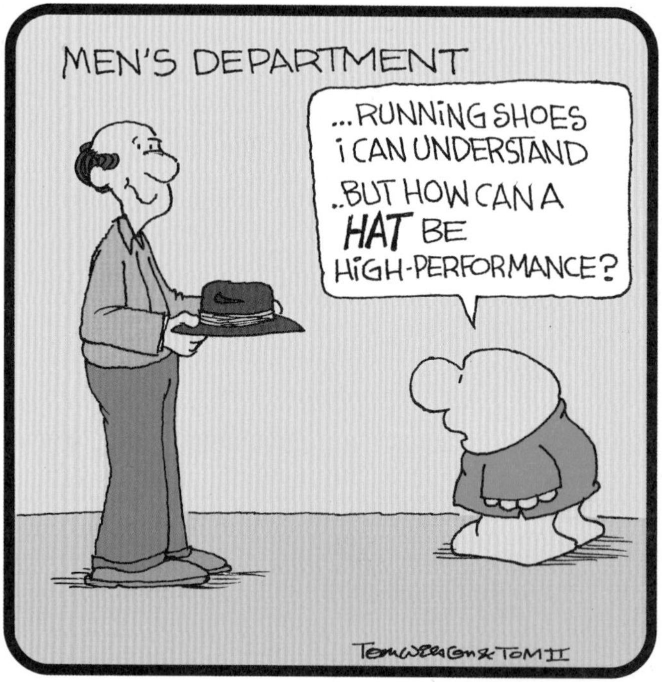
MEN'S DEPARTMENT
...RUNNING SHOES I CAN UNDERSTAND ..BUT HOW CAN A HAT BE HIGH-PERFORMANCE?
Tom Wilson & TOM II

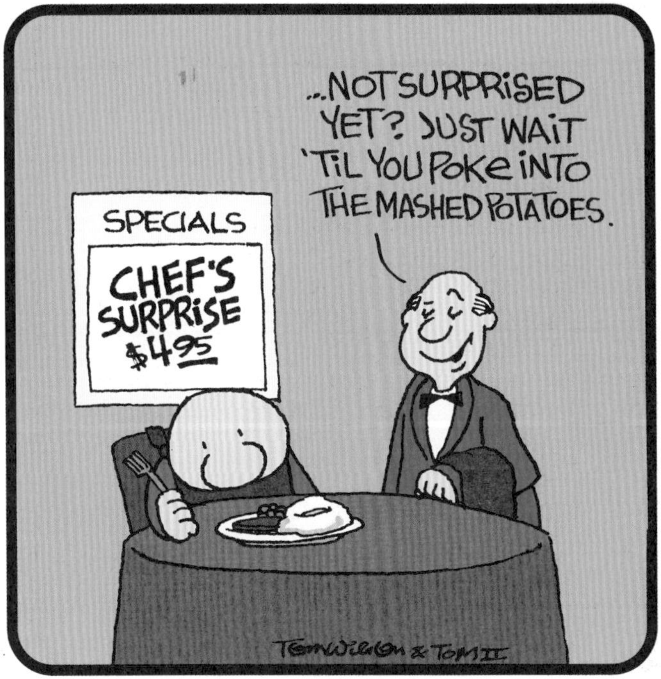
...NOT SURPRISED YET? JUST WAIT 'TIL YOU POKE INTO THE MASHED POTATOES.
SPECIALS
CHEF'S SURPRISE $4.95
Tom Wilson & Tom II

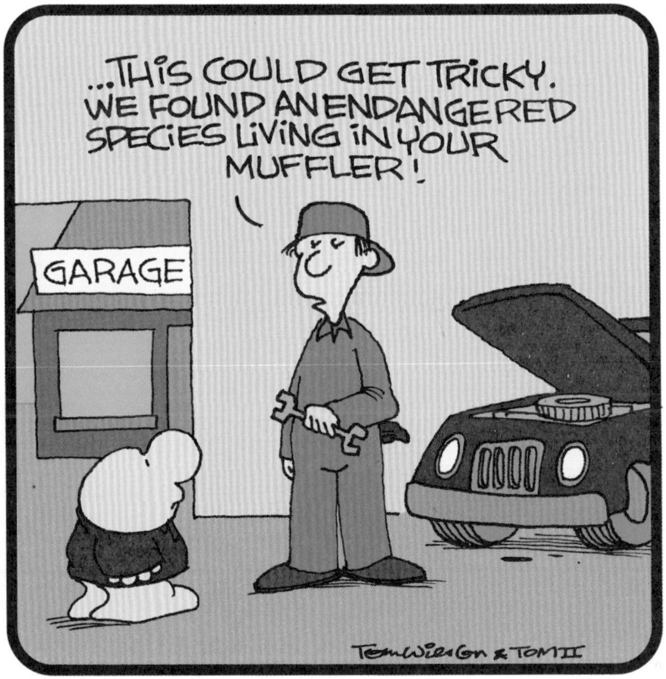
...THIS COULD GET TRICKY. WE FOUND AN ENDANGERED SPECIES LIVING IN YOUR MUFFLER!
GARAGE
Tom Wilson & Tom II

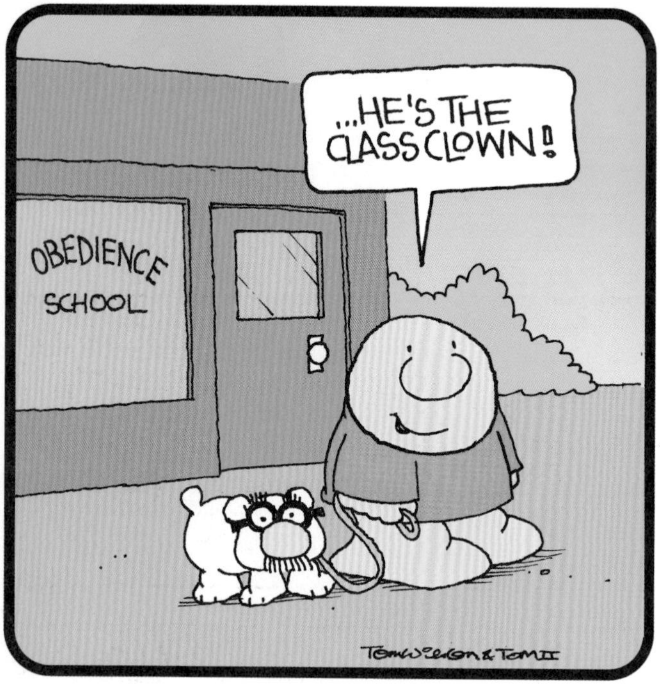
...HE'S THE CLASS CLOWN!
OBEDIENCE SCHOOL
TOM WILSON & TOM II

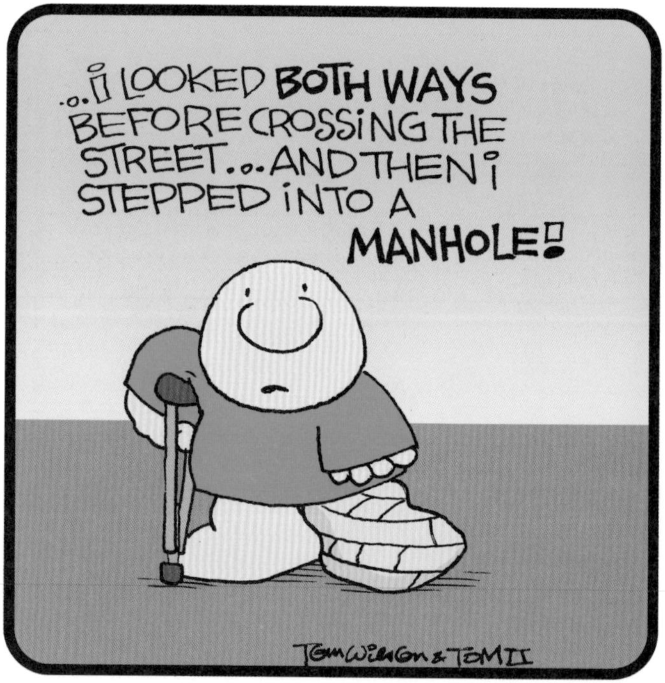
...I LOOKED **BOTH WAYS** BEFORE CROSSING THE STREET...AND THEN I STEPPED INTO A **MANHOLE!**
TOM WILSON & TOM II

-CLICK-
SPLORT!
..YOU'VE GOT TO BE CAREFUL WITH AEROSOL CHEESE!

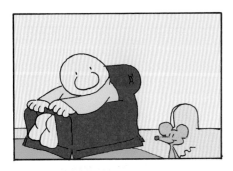

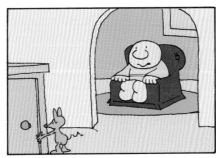

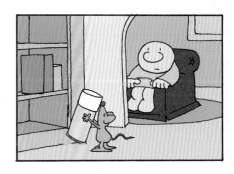

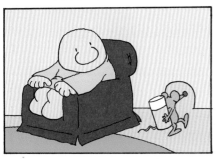

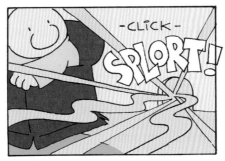

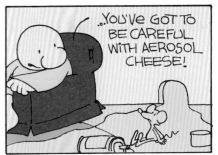

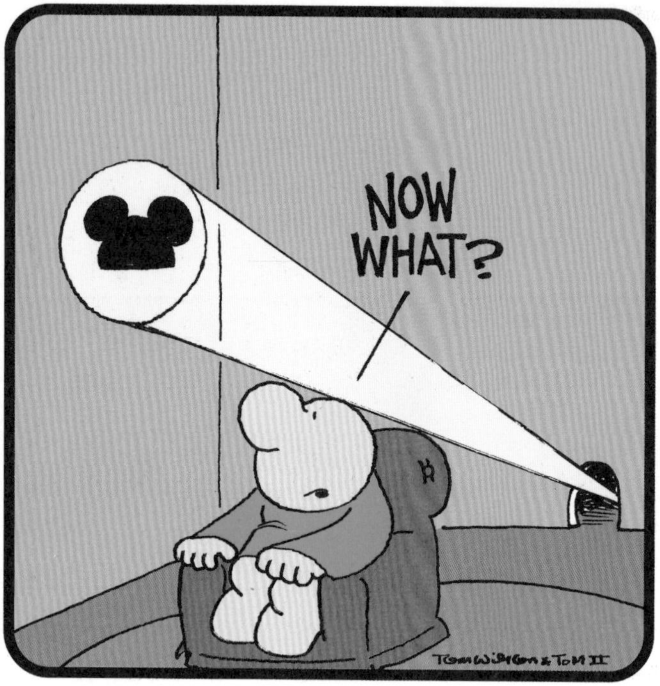
NOW WHAT?
TOM WILSON & TOM II

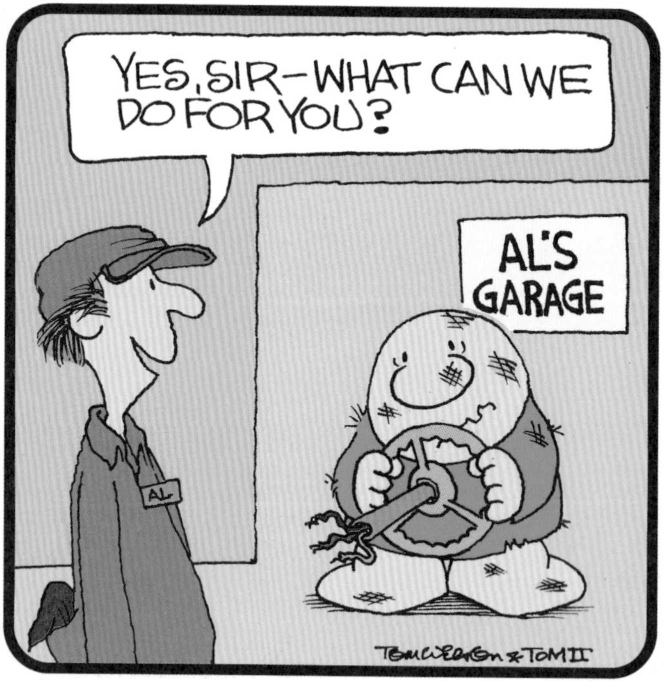
YES, SIR–WHAT CAN WE DO FOR YOU?
AL'S GARAGE
AL
TOM WILSON & TOM II

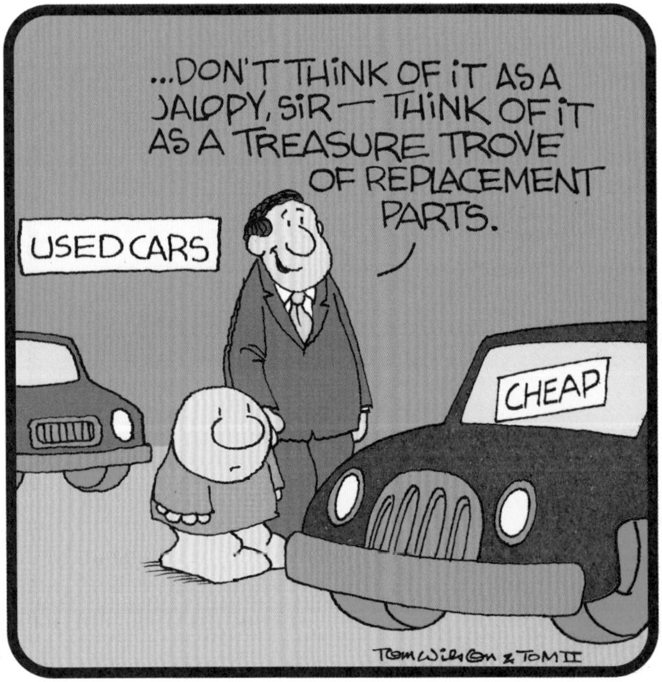
...DON'T THINK OF IT AS A JALOPY, SIR — THINK OF IT AS A TREASURE TROVE OF REPLACEMENT PARTS.
USED CARS
CHEAP
TOM WILSON & TOM II

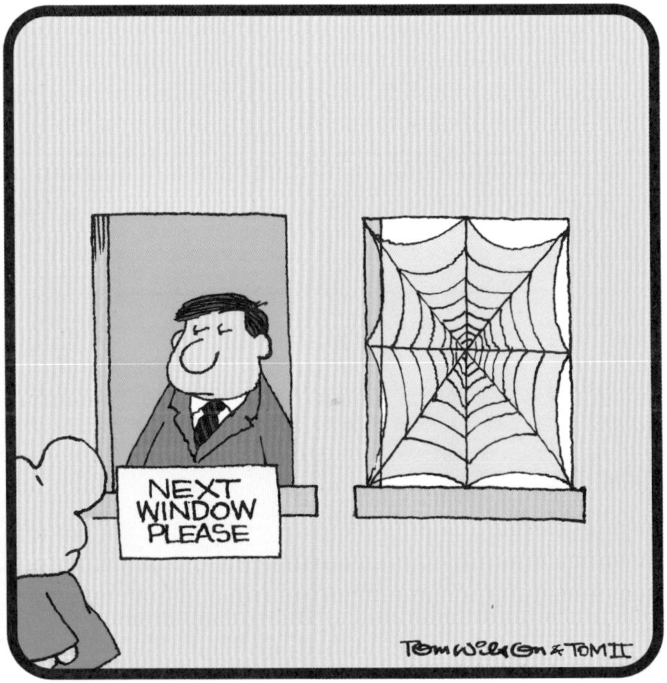
NEXT WINDOW PLEASE
TOM WILSON & TOM II

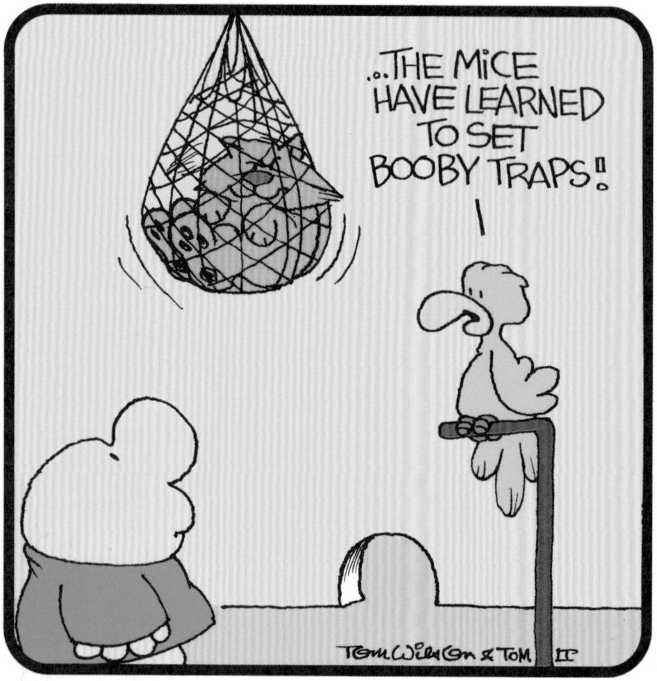
..THE MiCE HAVE LEARNED TO SET BOOBY TRAPS!
TOM WILSON & TOM II

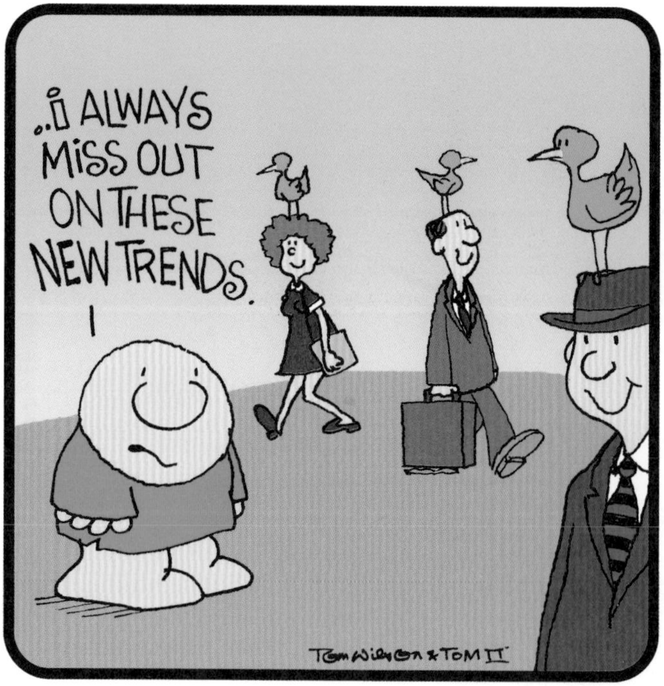
..i ALWAYS MiSS OUT ON THESE NEW TRENDS.
TOM WILSON & TOM II

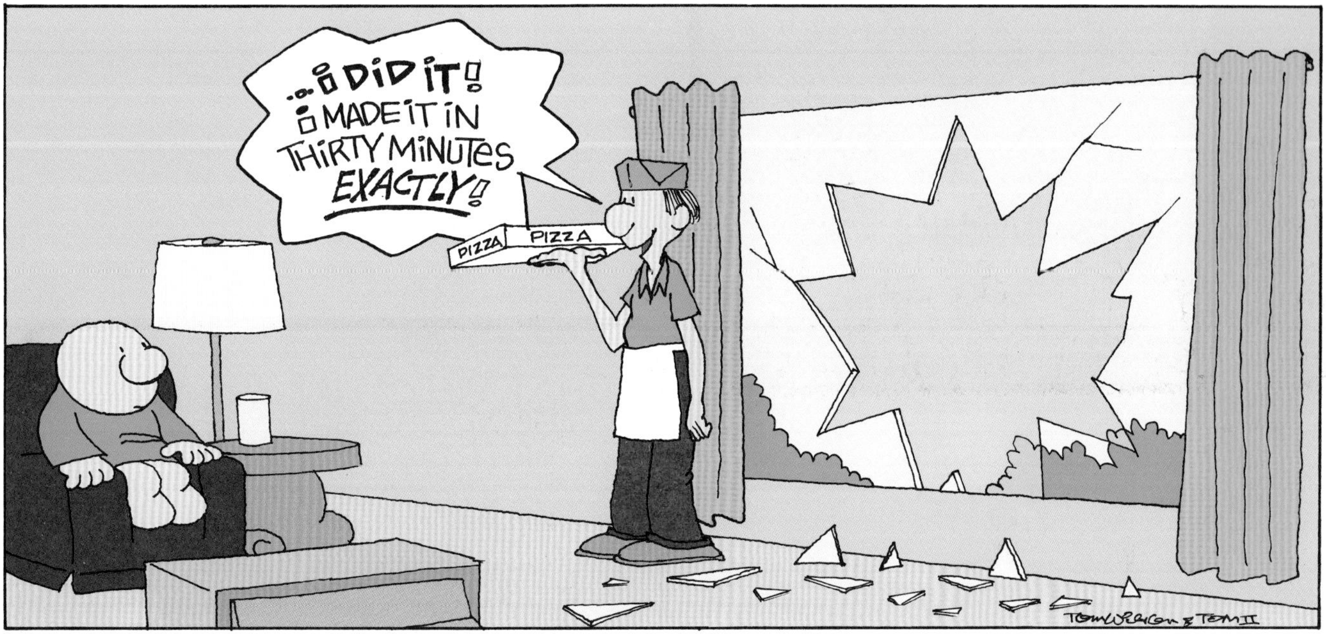
...I DID IT! I MADE IT IN THIRTY MINUTES EXACTLY!
PIZZA
PIZZA
TOM WILSON & TOM II

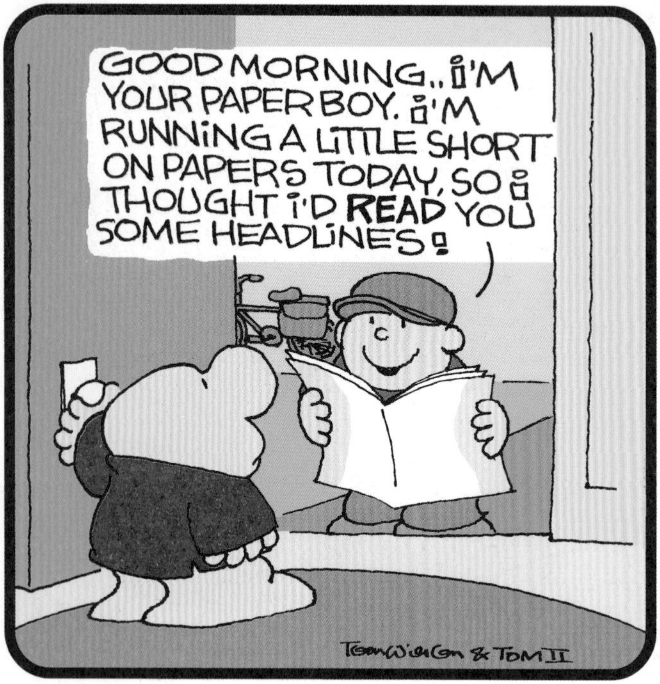
GOOD MORNING.. I'M YOUR PAPER BOY. I'M RUNNING A LITTLE SHORT ON PAPERS TODAY, SO I THOUGHT I'D **READ** YOU SOME HEADLINES!
Tom Wilson & TOM II

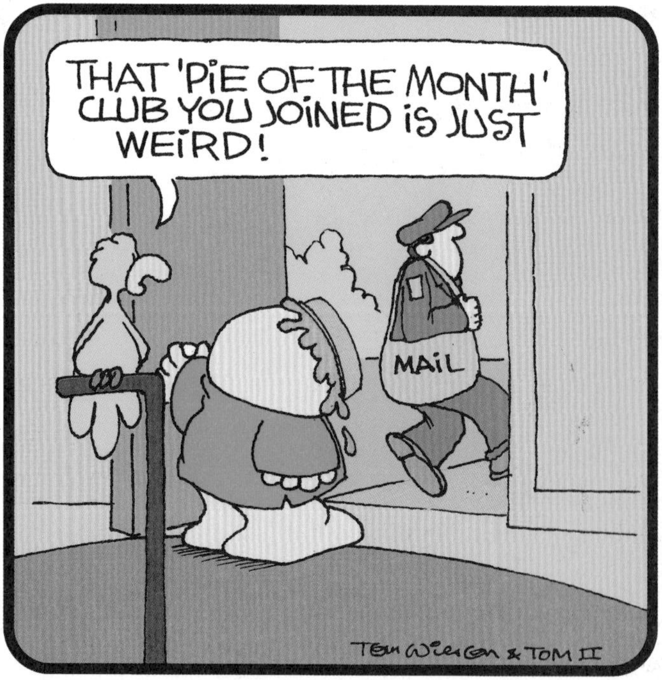
THAT 'PIE OF THE MONTH' CLUB YOU JOINED IS JUST WEIRD!
MAIL
Tom Wilson & TOM II

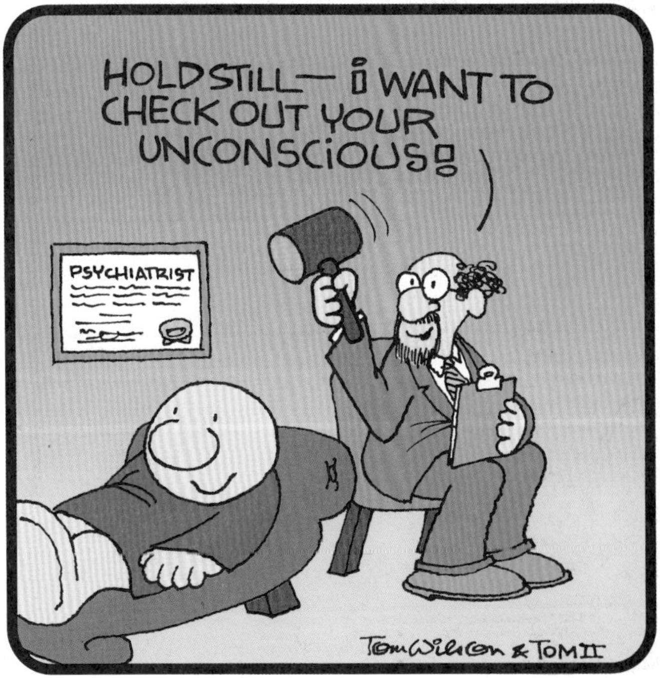
HOLD STILL— I WANT TO CHECK OUT YOUR UNCONSCIOUS!
PSYCHIATRIST
TOM WILSON & TOM II

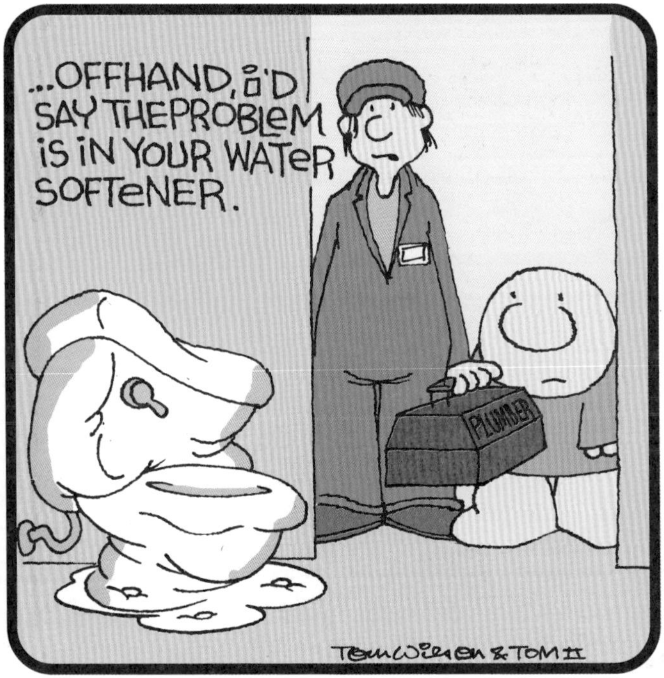
...OFFHAND, I'D SAY THE PROBLEM IS IN YOUR WATER SOFTENER.
PLUMBER
TOM WILSON & TOM II

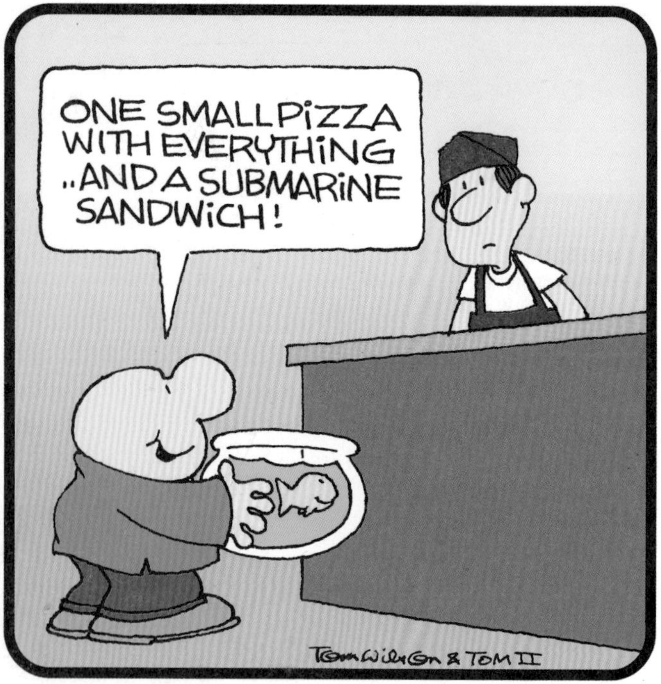
ONE SMALL PIZZA WITH EVERYTHING ..AND A SUBMARINE SANDWICH!
TOM WILSON & TOM II

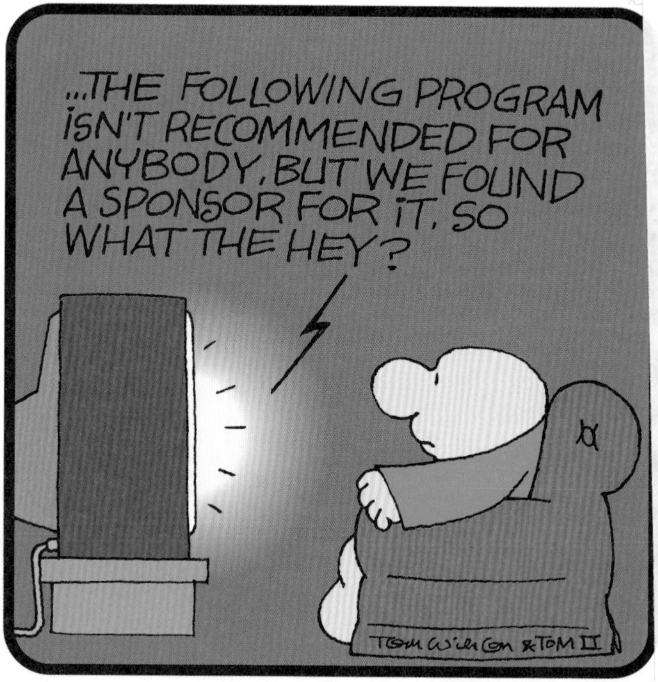
...THE FOLLOWING PROGRAM ISN'T RECOMMENDED FOR ANYBODY, BUT WE FOUND A SPONSOR FOR IT, SO WHAT THE HEY?
TOM WILSON & TOM II